This is the first of a 3-volume set on

PAUL BUNYAN

*I.   THE TALL TALES
II. THE LOGGING CAMPS
III. LEGEND ORIGINS

HISTORIC
HEARTLAND

Dedicated to my Home Town

BRAINERD

Capital of Paul Bunyan VACATIONLAND where it is not only the fish that are *BIG* and get *BIGGER* on retelling!

But also the home of:

Paul Bunyan Beard Contests begun 1925 . . .
Annual Paul Bunyan Expositions begun 1935 . . .
Johnny Inkslinker Crazy Days . . . a national novelty . . .

AND . . .

Famed, elaborate, exciting PAUL BUNYAN AMUSEMENT CENTER . . .
  Only thing of its kind in the World!
Ray Bang's PAUL BUNYAN AXEMEN of the Brainerd Rotary Club . . .
  A World "First" in Rotary International!
FIRST ANNUAL PAUL BUNYAN FESTIVAL September 1983 . . .
  World Premiere: Unique on the Upper Mississippi!
SECOND ANNUAL PAUL BUNYAN FESTIVAL September 1984 . . .
  World Premiere of this book!

AND . . .

8-foot statue of **Paul** and **Babe** built in 1935 . . .
  First in World so far as known!
40-foot **Paul Bunyan** animated with both voice and motion . . .
  Largest Paul Bunyan in the World!
50-ton (if filled with cement) **Babe the Blue Ox** . . .
  So who's going to argue with that?
134-foot **Golf Tee** used by Paul for his 19th hole . . .
  Amen!

FURTHERMORE . . .

Only 49.98 (bargain) miles from the home of **Paul's Sweetheart** in Hackensack!
Only 79.98 (bargain) miles from **Paul's Logging Camp** at Grand Rapids!
Only 99.98 (bargain) miles from the **Summer Home of Paul and Babe** in Bemidji!

For the rest: *"Come see, comme ça!!!* as Bull Cook "Froglegs" Chevalier in Paul's Camp Nine on the Androscoggin would say.

PAUL BUNYAN

VOLUME I

THE TALL TALES
AND THE WORLD'S FIRST BUNYAN BIOGRAPHY

by

Carl Andrew Zapffe

M.Sc., Sc.D., D.Eng'g. *Hon.*
Historian,
Historic Heartland Association

☆ *The first family biography on the all-time legendary hero of lumberjacks and logging camps!*

☆ *An anthology of legends and tales spun around the bunkhouse deacon seats of logging camps from Maine to Minnesota and West to Timbuktu – Plus a few more by the man who wrote the book!*

HISTORIC
HEARTLAND
ASSOCIATION, INC.

BRAINERD, MINNESOTA 56401

The Historic Heartland Association is a non-profit organization incorporated under laws of Minnesota, having as its first purpose the collecting and preserving of precious photographic and literary materials relating to the Lake Region of the Upper Mississippi, and as its general purpose the study, assimilation, and eventual publication of these materials for the education and enjoyment of future generations. *The Legend of Paul Bunyan* belongs to our historic heritage; and although this first volume goes beyond the usual definitions of history, the second volume will return the situation to normalcy by presenting a wealth of historic description in the form of a gallery of fascinating photographs taken from the Association's "Century Vault" – a novel scientifically designed storage system for photographic reproductions which will permit future generations to get as close to the original as possible – within one step. The third volume also engages in serious history, pursuant to tracing the origins and growth of this legend, the greatest in American folklore.

Yes, I promise – there will be only one *Tall Tales!*

Library of Congress Catalogue
Card No. 84-61337

ISBN 0-910623-02-3

Printed by Bang Printing Company, Brainerd, Minnesota 56401

WARNING TO READER:

Every race, and indeed every nation or tribe having any substantial depth of history, boasts a folklore. And what is folklore?

While we shall labor the answer to this quite complex question in a sequel volume, here it will suffice to say that *folklore* is the type of narration which (1) spans the entire spectrum from the factually real to the purely imaginary; (2) concerns alleged events too remote to permit checking; and (3) avoids all other possible criticism by hiding behind the skirts of the classical editorial "they say".

That is, until the very time of this book, nobody could ever point a finger at some lout spouting off on Bunyan and say: "*You* dunnit!" It's always hearsay. And even now the trap is only triggered by those parts where, for example, Bunyan is found raising a previously unmanufactured family so far as everybody's best information is concerned. Unquestionably, *nobody* has ever heard of GAZONK and his self-shucking oysters, his fable-producing brothers (one-third brothers?) Bully Belly B'hoy and Beautiful Legs Benson, neither their gorgeous Ojibwe mother 'Che-Washi-Wobble; and doughnuts will get you dollars that nobody in the entire Minnesota Northwest has ever really known from whence the commonly used term "Big Ten".

Yes, America is not only old enough to have its own folklore, Virginia dear, but its initiation and growth were understandably expedited to vast measure by the incredible series of events which only began with the discovery by Columbus of a totally new race of people. Even the Christian Church required ten months and a special encyclical from the Pope to accept the fact that the American Indian was a human being. The hallmark of *size* was then quickly stamped upon our folklore when it became known that Columbus had also discovered two totally new continents. Everything from that time on became big, bold, and boisterous, bulging the imagination until few could tell where truth ended and fiction began. Official reports described mermaids in the Caribbean, a merman in Lake Superior, one-eyed cyclops in the woods. Even Thomas Jefferson contributed his bit by raising a great commotion over the discovery of mastodon bones on our East Coast. As for the aspect of derring-do, anyone at all acquainted with real-life circumstances on the dramatic American frontier can hack that.

So America does indeed have a folklore; and among its myriad gems and facets, the diadem is the Bunyan Legend of the logging frontier. Whether or not Paul was ever real, the legend assuredly is; and because it's so interwoven with frontier history, the legend itself has become a subject of research in the Historic Heartland program. In fact, three sequel volumes are on the drawing board:

I. **The Tall Tales**
II. **The Logging Camps**
III. **Legend Origins**

In the next volume we go serious for a change of pace, with a beautiful picture gallery on historic logging operations; whereupon the research then winds up in a rather scholarly (?) fashion with an exhaustive literature review, a tracking down of the legend's origins, and an analysis of just what it is that not only brings forth such a preposterous legend, but continues to make it tick long after the 'jacks are gone.

But in this first we really let down the bars. Attention is confined entirely to the wild yarns themselves; and the collection contains the best of just about all that have ever been published – plus a few of our own. Those who might question the level of humor in some parts should bear in mind that this is a story of *lumberjacks* – exceedingly *macho* men living out their lives in the deep woods, not a meeting of the W.C.T.U. We have already trimmed the original out-of-the-woods stuff to leave material sufficient for another 3-volume set by some other writer. We made these deletions out of a great sense of respect for La Leche and the Future Mothers of America, the Boy Scouts of America, the Campfire Girls and Brownies, all innocent young female teenagers in the 4-H Clubs, and of course the S.P.C.A.

Believe it or not – and this *is* probably the last time in Volume I when you can trust the author – the object on the facing page *is* on the National Register of Historic Sites! But of course, not as Paul's Golf Tee.

Nevertheless, it does have an interesting historic connection with the present narrative, as well as its marvelous adaptability for a Bunyan foil. In the first place, it's big. Second, the location is fitting. For as far as the present research has been able to disclose, Brainerd was the first municipality to tee off the Bunyan Legend with a celebration, and the first to build a statue of Paul and Babe.

Third, there is another odd coincidence with this old abandoned water tower, now enjoying doubled fame for having held Brainerd's justly boasted "pure water". For it was devised and authorized by a geologist working for the Northern Pacific Railroad, in days when everybody believed a concrete tower would never take a Minnesota winter. This scientifically trained man believed otherwise; and the authority for proceeding with its construction arose from his serving as President of the Water and Light Board – purely as a sideline – for seventeen years at a salary of one dollar per year. This same geologist then proceeded to conduct experiments with the staining problem in Brainerd's water. For no laundress could come up with a clean shirt. When he found the answer, he secured a United States Patent and sold it to the City for one dollar. Result: *"Brainerd's Pure Water"*, produced in his special filtration plant which continues to do its job to this day.

That geologist was the the father of the present author.

PAUL BUNYAN'S GOLF TEE

AT BRAINERD, MINNESOTA
A nationally registered Historic Site.

USED FOR HIS 19th HOLE – AND HIS FAVORITE DRINK:

BRAINERD'S PURE WATER!

Special photo by Steve Kohls (July '84) Courtesy Brainerd Daily Dispatch.

TABLE OF CONTENTS

PREFACE

So we did it, and we're glad.

For years this writer has wanted to gather into one place the principal Bunyan stories – those worthy of preservation, that is – and to render the whole legend in a more or less coherent form. The idea of adding a few embellishments arose out of natural inclinations to blow everything out of their true proportions; and this came to a head in the Summer of 1981 when attending luncheon meetings of the Brainerd Rotary Club. As one of those honorary Club members dubbed "Paul Bunyan Axeman" – a Brainerd novelty unique throughout the Rotary world – I arose at a Tuesday noon luncheon and, when asked the usual question about professional classification and home club, replied:

"Oyster Shucking, Baltimore, Maryland!"

Naturally, this required some explanation; and thus was "Little Gazonk" born. For nobody had ever proposed, or even hinted, that Paul's brain in any way matched his physique. The popular image instead is more that of the dinosaur – tons of flesh manipulated with button-size brain power. BUT – Paul might have had a kid where the size hormones, chromosomes, genes or pheromes went to grey matter instead of muscle? Ya? Ya, gewiss! Achtung! Bingo!

So what might a small kid with an oversize brain come up with? To hell with chess, Rubik's cube, and speed-reading – Bunyan was a practical person; and it is a matter of common dictionary-level knowledge that Paul was simply *wild* over oysters, particularly those from the Chesapeake Bay.

Well, so why should one go through all the tantalizing miseries and outright physical dangers of shucking oysters with the traditional shucking knife when, merely by hooking up the spark coil from some old Model-T Ford, then lightly touching friend *Mollusca* with the electrodes both fore and aft, teeth and arss, you could instantaneously influence him to get the hellouta there – all by himself, yes, and *but fast!* Simple stuff for anyone trained to think.

Over the course of a subsequent series of luncheons I was understandably called upon to bring this exciting story of Gazonk and his oyster-shucking on Chesapeake Bay up to date. When summer was finally over, and the chill was on the pumpkin in Minnesota, the sheer inertia of the Gazonk yarn brought it all the way to the sunny island of Jost Van Dyke in the British Virgins where I had gone to do some undisturbed writing on jet-engine metallurgy. Little Gazonk was simply on an inventive kick; and when rained in one weekend, out he came as an interesting pastime.

Yes, present intentions do include giving a somewhat scholarly review of the literary and bibliographic situation relative to our remarkable All-American, **Paul Bunyan.** For the legends surrounding this redoubtable if mythical figure actually comprise the most dynamic and extensive body of materials to be found in all of American folklore! Yes indeedy, Paul has full credentials in every college and university having a Department of American Folklore. We also propose to make available to the enjoyment of history buffs in particular and everybody in general the remarkable gallery of historic photographs showing logging camps and lumberjack life from the Century Vault collection of the Historic Heartland Association.

However, this serious stuff would kill the Fun Bird before it ever got off the pot. So we shall lay it aside for sequel volumes and hit the sideshow first. This immediately brings us to a few acknowledgments and confessions. As for the acknowledgments: First and foremost, the manuscript by itself would go over like a molybdenum-uranium balloon if it were not for the cartoons. So to my clever son-in-law José Vielma and his remarkable associates acknowledged inside the front cover goes the Blue Ribbon, the 19-gun salute – and perhaps the Paul Bunyan Purple Heart, depending upon our reception. In fact, some of their cartoons are likely to become classics; at the very least, they will present future writers with a tough act to follow.

As for the confessions: Having some sensitivity despite appearances of the present text, I am most anxious to point out that in putting together this collection of Bunyan lore, I have necessarily engaged in wholesale plagiarism. Two great difficulties impede a proper confession: First, the tales have been so bandied about and loosely treated by predecessors, I really do not know exactly whom to acknowledge for what. None of the illustrations belongs to others, but many of the animal descriptions do. And I have tried to enter references and scattered remarks acknowledging such standouts as the books of Cox, Wyman, and Carson, plus a few others. But this unexpectedly mushrooming research – quickly running over a hundred titles of books and articles – simply had to stop somewhere, so it stopped short of discovering who copyrighted what. I myself will accordingly take a generous stand regarding anybody using the present stuff.

Second, the relatively uninhibited presentation has generally butchered original stories so badly we are probably more subject to charges of misrepresentation than plagiarism. It is almost advisable not to let the reader know where the story came from, lest a derogatory image attach to the originator. Let me pull the pucker strings for closing this bewildering and somewhat embarrassing bag by paraphrasing that great scientist Sir Isaac Newton, who in his characteristically modest manner said:

> If perchance the present work might elevate the writer to the position of the world's greatest liar, it is only because I have stood on the shoulders of giants who have gone before me.

So let's get on with the show!

C. Andrew Z.

Paul Bunyan Axeman
Brainerd Rotary Club

CHRONOLOGY:

Launch: Sandy Ground Estates, Jost Van Dyke, B.V.I., Christmas 1981

Space Walk: Royal Palms Condo, Grand Cayman, W.I., Ides of March, 1983

Land: Holiday Beach Resort, Longboat Key, FL, Mother's Day 1983

Edit: CAZlab, Baltimore, MD, Father's Day, 1984

Press: Villa Z, So. St. Colombo, Gull Lake, MN, 72nd Birthday, 7/25/84

CHAPTER I

HOW IT ALL BEGAN

*(*Superscript numbers refer to references at the close of each Chapter.)*

In faraway Kennebunkport, Maine – some *szu tusend* years ago says "River Rat" Ole Olson – one of Maine's great lumberjacks had a son who was already big, and who then grew so much bigger from eating beans in the camp chow that it was utterly ridiculous. He simply became blown out of all proportions.

Nobody remembers how or why a kid ever got into a lumbercamp, neither does anybody remember his actual name, if he ever had one. But brother! how they remember his deeds! The Bluenose Brainerd Legend[1] has it that he arrove by balloon from Nova Scotia and landed in a camp in the Valley of the Chippewa River in Wisconsin. Biographer Brown[2] claims that he was the 'Tit Jean or Petit Jean, also called Bon Jean, born on Prince Edward Island in the Gulf of St. Lawrence; that for his baptism he was lowered by a crane into Malpeque Bay, the great splash causing those tidal waves in the Bay of Fundy

State of Maine
City of Bangor

Record of Birth

Name of Child	PAUL BUNYAN
Date of Birth	February 13, 1834
Place of Birth	Bangor, Maine
Father's Name	Jaques Bunyan
Father's Birthplace	Bangor, District of Maine
Mother's Maiden Name	Sarah Marie DuBois
Mother's Birthplace	Bangor, District of Maine
Date Recorded	February 18, 1834

State of Maine

Penobscot s.s.   Bangor, August 25, 1982
I hereby certify that the foregoing is a true copy from the Record of Births for the City of Bangor.
Witness my hand and Seal of the said City.

Russell J. McKenna   City Clerk.

Official (?) Certificate of the Birth of Paul Bunyan in Bangor, Maine, the World's Lumber Capital of the Mid-Nineteeth Century.

Courtesy Mr. and Mrs. Kenneth Baird
and Bangor City Clerk Russell J. McKenna

Blessed bundle from . . . ???

which have not subsided yet; and that when he yelled his objection to the unceremonious dunking, the entire fishing fleet of Nova Scotia put out to sea thinking their comrades were in distress. His voice was generally described as a cross between the braying of a barnfull of jackasses and three buzz-saws cutting oak – with a bass drum thrown in for the glottal catch. Grateful Nova Scotians still remember him for the time a fly landed on his nose, causing him to make his first sneeze, which stopped the approach of a terribly threatening storm and blew it the other way. Ungrateful Londoners remember him because they were the other way. Canadians remember him for the problems he gave the women making his diapers and clothes. The looms got so hot they had to do their weaving under Niagara Falls; and the best they could do for buttons was to use old wagon wheels.

During the mid-19th Century there was little question that Bangor, Maine, was the Lumber Capital of the World; and the Chamber of Commerce in that fascinating city, home of Joe Peavey's famous Peavey Improved Cant-Dog[3], claims to have Paul's birth certificate, which we reproduce here. But as much as Minnesotans respect the famed loggers of Maine, who taught us most our log larnin', both the location and date are ridiculous. Even a Boy Scout can tell you that Paul came from several weeks northwest of Quebec, and was born at least 15 feet before there ever was a 19th Century.

Even worse, unfortunately, is the alleged Marriage License some of our own beloved Minnesotans have published[4], claiming a marriage of Paul 9 June 1838 to a girl in the then Iowa Territory. For the dam geographic coordinates they give, namely 46°50′ *longitude* and 94°30′ *latitude*, would place the

"MUSH! dammit **MUSH!**"

ceremony 4°30′ in outer space beyond the North Pole!

Of course, Paul *was* a bit unusual . . .

So many cities such as Bemidji[5] claim to be Paul's birthplace, for one illegitimate reason or another, that he must have been a crowd rather than a man. Brainerd would seem to have some claim because of that city's archaeological records of Paul Bunyan Beard Contests beginning as early as 1925, and the neolithic 8-foot statue of Paul and Babe that Art Lyonais had made[6] for their First Annual Paul Bunyan Exposition[7] in 1935. This is the earliest statuary known to the present study, being two years before the Bemidji masterpiece, and a full quarter-century prior even to that in Bangor, Maine[8].

Nevertheless, that fair dwelling place of saints and sinners, gateway to the gorgeous lake region of the Mississippi headwaters, self-proclaimed Capital of Paul Bunyan Vacationland, home of pure water and the battle ground for fluoridation, simply records[7] in its characteristically modest manner that a male child was delivered – somewhere, obviously – by five large storks working overtime; that already at the age of one week he was wearing his father's clothes; and that the family had the misfortune of hiring a nurse who was not very well educated. She could only count to 22 by using her fingers, toes, and ears; and one day while the child was eating his buckets of porridge, he went right on to 56 and got sick. So his mother fired the nurse and invented the card-index system to keep track of the boy's diet. Eventually this would become the Fortran IV program for the IBM 390/91. They used a lumberwagon for his carriage, though they had to tie down his arms to keep him from waving them about in his babyish way, and flattening fences or knocking over trees when giggling with delight at the sight of a tornado. They also had to lash his legs to the buckboard so they didn't hang off the rear and tear up the roadbed. But this was really not Paul's fault; his feet were so far away he rarely saw them.

Whatever the facts may be, and whatever his real name might have been, so many generations of loggers have since sat on their buns either around the bunkhouse stove or outdoors around campfires, spinning yarns about the famed and incredible character, that he came rather naturally to be identified with those BUN YARNS; and over the thousands of years of language evolution since the last Great Ice Age, the Mankato Maximum of 9564 B.C.[9], that identification became his name. At some unknown later date it was shortened to BUNYAN. Nevertheless, scientific accuracy in this our own Space Age requires recognition of that etymological antecedent *Bun Yarn* for any of those fascinating tales told in so many lands about the World's Greatest Lumberjack.

No record whatever is at hand to explain his rather ordinary and seemingly Christian monicker *Paul*; but it is generally assumed that it belongs to the famous *Legend of the Bull Cook*. All major logging camps within range of our recorded history have had a Head Cook or Master Cook, with or without a "slush cook" backup, plus one or more helpers

The Bull Cook guillotine.

3

variously called cookees, flunkies, or taffles. The man called the Bull Cook was really no cook at all, but rather the bunkhouse janitor, and the man in charge of feeding the other animals – the animals in the barn.

Nevertheless, in those early days now in question, the camps knew no such luxury as a kitchen staff; and it was accordingly the Bull Cook, or else. Furthermore, he not only prepared the meal, but it was his dangerous task to call the men to lunch as well. Usually there was a special hole built in the kitchen wall so Cookee could stick his head out, holler: "CHOW!", then pull it back in before it got sheared off in the rush. The French Revolution of 1791 tried to use this general idea; but the polite Frenchman differs so much from the lumberjack that they had to invent the guillotine instead. However, let us return to Paul.

When the youngster was still too young to have any teeth, and his vocabulary was largely limited to sheer noise, there was an historic character doing the cooking in Camp 9, who would shortly become known as the late and lamented Bull Cook Benson. Benson was built like a real brick Chic Sales 3-holer; and his neck muscles were so elastic and strong that for 17 years he had kept both his head and his job, and to hell with the camp guillotine. On the day now in question, however, Benson made his first mistake – leaving him only one more to go, according to his epitaph. He came out of the kitchen with the big camp kettle filled with beans, and asked the Kid how much he wanted shoveled on his plate.

Now, what the child meant to say was undoubtedly: "PUT IT ALL!" And how his childish mind *thought* this should sound was probably: "PUD'ALL!"; whereas what actually came out was:

"P'ALL!!!"

Initiation of the Benson Syndrome.

It was just that simple – except that every bean in the pot took flight – right into cookee's face! Now of course getting hit in the face with a load of beans flying just below Mach 1 is not fatal, though it did leave Benson with a terrible case of acne for the rest of his short life. In fact, those beans which were driven in too deeply tended to sprout if Benson didn't wash his face. This was not only an annoyance to Benson, because he had to prune his face as well as shave it, but it made even the lumberjacks sick to their stomachs if the sprouts got too long.

One thing about the kid's bean diet was that it kept blowing his diapers off. Now, while this did have the advantage of usually drying them out before they landed, it kept the chore boy busy running them down. So Bellows Bologna, the old Italian blacksmith of Camp 9, in his ever-trusting but simple way, tried to be helpful one day by riveting them on. Unfortunately, the result was that they first blew full like a spinnaker on a racing scow, and then both Kid and

diaper took off right over the trees and away. Fortunately he landed in one of the camp's cutting areas, though the occasion proved a bit strange. In the first place, a crew of Swedes from the Old Country, working under Swamper Swanson, happened to look up just as Paul went sailing overhead; and this they found very difficult to understand. It made matters no easier that they knew very little English, because it would be difficult to explain such a thing even with alot of English.

Second, when Kid came down, he landed in the top of a huge white pine running some 3000 board feet, and just as it was being felled by a pair of Norwegians pulling a Tuttle-tooth crosscut. "TIMBER!" they yelled – and down came Kid, complete with diapers. These Norwegians couldn't understand that either; and for the next two days both of them passed out cigars in blue wrappers to the whole crew, thinking they had fathered a fine boy.

"Kid" visits fellers!

So far as Benson's bean acne was concerned, sweet oblivion soon came to the rescue. The youngster was now nearly 3 years old, and beans simply had to go, so far as his diet was concerned. It was weaning time. We know the date was exactly the 30th of March; but the rather emotional lumberjacks who buried their beloved Bull Cook, buried the year with him, so there wasn't any year that year.

Anyway, it seems the faithful Benson had decided to wean the Kid on beef; and for that he barbecued a whole bull. Then, never supposing for a moment that a bull situation had any relationship whatever to a bean situation, be absentmindedly asked his young friend the same question:

"How much do you want?"

So this was Benson's second and last mistake, and those were his famous very last words. For there is a world of difference between being hit in the face with a load of beans, and getting rushed by a hot bull. He was buried with the simple but touching ceremonies typical of lumber camps: dig, dump, cover, and go back to work. Then that evening the 'Jacks gathered in solemn convocation, around the empty mess tables which made the occasion so solemn; and they decided they must not only hire a new cook, but one with a better life guarantee. Yes, they would hire a Head Cook, and then get a Bull Cook for his assistant – and one who was definitely expendable.

Four years of relative quiet passed, except for Kid getting a bad case of mumps. It took three doctors, an osteopath, several chiropractors, and one mind-reader, also three duck hunters, to pull him through.

In fact, it was the duck hunters who really stemmed the disease. Apparently because the Mump Bugs were feasting on such an unusual Kid, they grew so big that the hunters were able to shoot them down as they flew from tonsil to tonsil. Interestingly enough, this not only became the first time that anybody had actually seen a Mump Bug, but it opened the whole modern approach to the understanding of infectious diseases in terms of a bug or virus. After Paul's time, however, they had to wait for the invention of the microscope in order to see them again.

At the time next in question, Kid was teething; and he had lost his two front teeth. A new Bull Cook just arrived, replacing No. 3. For it seems No. 1 worked out fine for a couple whole months, but then suffered a direct hit when changing Paul's diapers, the autopsy showing death by drowning. The second simply couldn't hack it, and quit in time to save his life; while the third got squashed all over the table top when Kid mistook him for a fly and gave him a swat.

So comes now No. 4, the big stolid Finn Evil Evold; and before his campmates had time to warn him, he politely sought the Kid's preferences – hindquarters or forequarters? Once again the Benson Syndrome:

"P'ALL!!!"

Unfortunately, Paul was now so much larger it meant more than just a long line of hungry 'Jacks holding empty plates and going without dinner – much more. In the first place, the blast focusing through the gap in his teeth reached such an enormous concentration of power it knocked every Mother's son among them flat on the floor, then blew the south wall out of the cookhouse. Second,

Medication for mumps . . . shooting down "kid's" mump bugs.

"Kid" is rapidly becoming known as "P'ALL!"

6

while Evil Evold did recover sufficiently by Tuesday to go about his business serving chow, the concussion from being slapped in the face by a barbecued bull naturally left him somewhat stupefied. And believe it or not, he now opened his big rubbery gub and asked that same stupid question again! This was the penultimate or next-to-the-last Benson Syndrome, and it was a real disaster. The loggers had just moved into a brand new camp; and Paul's reply leveled the whole pinery before the men got a chance to cut a single stick.

By now the frightful experiences were so ingrained in everybody's memory that nobody – but nobody – ever asked Kid how much he wanted. They just ran in the wheelbarrows and dumped it on the railroad flatcar that he used for a dinner plate.

Almost nobody, that is. For there was that one last event in recorded history when one of the 'Jacks themselves, trying to appear helpful in the eyes of the Walking Boss during an inspection of the camp, turned to Paul and popped the fatal question of the Benson Syndrome. By now the lad had grown another six fathoms, and each tooth weighed about a Scotch stone. The really striking feature of this particular situation, however, was not the sudden departure of the Walking Boss, but rather that the blast caught the Section Foreman Sven Johannsen while he was cleaning up for dinner. For at that very moment Sven was delicately perched on the camp's rustic but hygienic "roasting pole". Catching the full blast in such a favorable position for launch, the big Scandihoovian instantly took off and was soon in full orbit.

Since the dyed-in-wool Lumberjack is related to the elephant along three lines of Darwinian evolution instead of the usual two, he never forgets. And to this day their greatest Folk Hero is not only "P'ALL" to them, now usually distorted to **Paul** by an unbelieving generation, but it makes the blood of every mother's son among them boil to hear credit given to the Russians for putting the first man in space.

For not only did the 'Jacks beat the Russians to it by thousands of years, thanks to Paul, but they are still waiting for their beloved Foreman Sven to come back to Camp 9.

Sven Johannsen's historic Pre-Apollo launch from the Camp Nine "Roasting Pole."

REFERENCES

1. Brown, C. E.: *Bluenose Brainerd Stories*, Wisconsin Folklore Soc., Madison, Wisc. 5 pp. (1943)
2. Brown, C. E.: *Paul Bunyan and Tony Beaver Tales*, Pub. by author, Madison, Wisc. 18 pp. (1930)
3. Baird, K. & M.: Personal Correspondence (1982); Peavey's blacksmith shop, where the tool originated, was in Stillwater, Maine; but Bangor became the big production center.
4. Kading, G. and Burnson, W.: *The Hackensack Sweetheart Story*, prepared for the Festival Committee, Hackensack, Mn., 20 pp. (July 1979); also see W. Burnson: *Legends Grow with Sweetheart Days*, Brainerd Daily Dispatch, Brainerd, MN., p. 8 (11 July 1982)
5. *Here's Your Story of Paul Bunyan from Bemidji, Minnesota*, Paul Bunyan's Headquarters, Bemidji Chamber of Commerce, 4 pp. folder (ca. 1983)
6. *Brainerd Landmark*, Brainerd Daily Dispatch, Brainerd, MN. p. 6 (16 Dec. 1980)
7. *Brainerd, Minnesota – The Capital of Paul Bunyan Playground Presents First Annual Brainerd Paul Bunyan Exposition*, Souvenir Program, 18 pp. (18-20 July 1935)
8. *Bangor's Paul Bunyan*, Greater Bangor Chamber of Commerce, Bangor, ME 04401 (ca. 1982)
9. Zapffe, C. A.: *A New Theory for the Great Ice Ages*, Physics Today **7**, No. 10, 14-7 (1954); disc. **7**, No. 12, p. 27 (1954)

CHAPTER II

PAUL'S EARLY YEARS

So *Paul* it was, and *Bunyan* the species, or family name. But let us return briefly to his baby days to flesh out our story.

As just indicated, it remains an unfathomable mystery just why a baby boy should land in a logging camp. Worse, nobody has ever said "Boo!" about his mother – if indeed he ever had a mother. Besides the questionable Bangor birth certificate, there was just that one carefully repeated legend that he came by way of five storks; and it is said that the storks worked 12-hour shifts for three days, also that the days themselves were big in those days – 60 hours long instead of the usual 24, which accounts for the five

Liddo Paul gets him liddo-diddums first toothums.

storks taking 12-hour shifts.

Certainly it had never happened before, nor has it ever happened since. The engineering aspects of his arrival alone were perfectly horrendous, requiring a rigging called the Brainerd Truss[1], which was later used for bridges in New England before invention of the Howe Truss; and perhaps this strange omen foretold the eventual location of Paul Bunyan Vacationland in a city named after another later member of that same Brainerd family which boasts the invention of this ancient rigging on Paul's first diaper.

Once he was in camp, of course, a special bottle had to be built to feed this "precious bundle" from nobody knows where. The same dear blacksmith who later riveted on his diapers, Bellows Bologna, accomplished this in short order by welding two bathtubs face to face and sticking the drain pipes down the Kid's hatch. Two whole barnfulls of double-udder Guernseys were then required to keep the thing going, one by day and one by night, with a third standing by to replace cows fretting from worn-out equipment.

At age one, and just when all the loggers were gathered around to celebrate his birthday, Paul performed the first of those stunning feats, at least so far as camp life was concerned, which would ever after mark his life: His first tooth broke through, with an acoustical shockwave that put out the candle! This was generally regarded as a strange omen; and some even claimed it shook the leaves off a nearby tree.

At age two his teeth were coming through so fast they had to hire a second blacksmith just to keep knocking the extra ones off with a hammer, lest he look like an alligator. And it was only one year later – at his third birthday party – that "little" Paul himself grabbed a peavey – that special lumberman's tool with both spike and dog at the end of a long pole – to pick the cake out of his teeth.

At age 5 he began developing the famous booming voice which led to the invention of the ear-muff. At first the loggers used the muffs to throttle down the blast and protect their ears from the noise; but when they later found it also kept their ears warm in cold weather, they just left them on. Furthermore, there was always the possibility that Paul might come back.

As we will recall, when Paul lost his two front teeth, he blew out the south wall of the loghouse used for the dining area. But it was not until shortly after his twelfth year that he made his first great display of physical strength. In those days of horse-drawn teams, the crooked roads that resulted from shifting the cutting crews from grove to grove proved a great drain on both team time and horse power. So Paul, in his playful kiddish way, would simply go out after breakfast and pull the roads straight.

Paul was very fast on his feet: He could blow out the lamps at one end of the bunkhouse and get into his sleeper before it got dark. He was also a great jumper, being able to leap any river in no more than three jumps. His eyes were so keen he could see all the way to the Rockies with only three or four looks, taking about one a week. Other 'Jacks had perfect 20/20 vision, but Paul's was 50/50. With just one eye

Paul's first job at camp – pulling the roads straight.

he could see half of everything, and with the other eye the other half. So what's left? This keen sight made him one of the best game trackers in the camp; and oldtimers still like to tell how young Paul once came upon the skeleton of a moose that had died of old age, then tracked him back to the place he was born.

Once, however, it seemed Paul's eyesight failed him. For he kept shooting at a deer that stuck its head up over a pile of brush. It took 28 shots before Paul finally knocked it down so it didn't come back up – or so he thought, till he went around the brush pile to get the critter and found he had killed an entire herd of 28 deer.

When all that venison was brought back to camp, there was widespread rejoicing; and Bellows Bologna decided he would reward Paul by building him a

special shotgun for the goose season shortly at hand. This worked out pretty well, except that Paul shot geese that were so high most of them spoiled before hitting the ground.

Like all other boys, Paul took his turn at school, though it didn't turn out so well. In the first place, he needed a special sheet of limestone from the Blackduck formation for his writing slate, with a charred white-pine log for a pencil. When the teacher had him write the numbers 1, 2, 3 . . . on his slate, she scolded him and sent him home because all the figures looked like a "1". But this was really the fault of the teacher, who couldn't see far enough to spot the curves. Paul never did learn how to write; and in later days he always had to draw pictures when ordering camp supplies. Once he ordered a new set of grindstones, but got a wagonload of cheese because

Paul forgets to sketch in the holes on his order for grinding wheels.

he forgot to draw in the holes.

About the only good thing to come out of Paul's schooling was the invention of the sandwich, which came about in this wise: One day the Slush Cook dumped two loaves of bread, one ham, a head of lettuce, a gallon of dill pickles, and a block of cheese into the washtub that Paul used for a lunch bucket. Trying to get more height out of his school stool, so's he could dangle his legs like other kids, he put the tub on top – then sat on it, producing the world's first sandwich. When the loggers discovered this new talent, they sent Paul up to sit on the roofs of new buildings, which squeezed the logs together so they didn't need chinking.

Soon Paul dropped out of school and stayed home instead to help his Dad in the potato garden. This was fortunate because it brought his inventive genius to light: Finding he got a sore toe from kicking out the potatoes, he invented the famed Safety Shoe with the metal plate in front. This in turn allowed him to kick out potatoes so fast that his Dad was able to plant three crops each year. Some trouble developed, however, with a few choice potatoes he kicked too far. For example, the one that got stuck on top of the torch of the Statue of Liberty did not set too well with Congress, since it gave immigrants the wrong idea of America. Any potato on a torch is presumably half-baked.

After his new set of teeth was fully in, Paul discovered to his chagrin that he could no longer whistle. But he quickly solved this by hollowing out a big dead Norway and making himself a flute. The music he came up with was even more beautiful than his whistling – to the general delight of the 'Jacks, and except for the fact that his high notes often knocked cockroaches and mice off the rafters into their soup, and even the needles off the pine trees. But this turned out to be a good thing. For in those days many of the logging contracts were on lands belonging to Indian reservations, where cutting was limited to "dead or down" timber. By getting Paul to play the *Star Spangled Banner*, every tree on the Reservation immediately looked either dead or down.

One Sunday afternoon just outside the bunkhouse Paul got so carried away with his flute-playing that he "ran the scales" for an encore, and all the shakes slid off the roof. Up till that time they had been called shingles.

Some of the harder-hearing of the men thought they should probably do something for the lad's musical development; and it just so happened that one of them had learned of a German band which recently went bankrupt. So they bought up all the instruments and gave them to Bellows Bologna to weld into one.

Unfortunately, what they did not know was that a colony of bumblebees had built their hive in the bassoon, and a pair of screech owls were sleeping out a tough night in the tuba. Accordingly, when Paul blew his first blow, there resulted a noise such as had never been heard before by human kind, and which ultimately resulted in the invention of the saxophone.

Many a ship captain, thinking the distant blast was a foghorn warning, sailed up the St. Lawrence instead of putting out to sea; and one unfortunate

Paul's flute was cute – for a telephone pole!

But his playing gave everything the shakes
(formerly called shingles)

schooner, which happened to be in direct line of the draft, was blown all the way around the Cape of Good Hope even with sails furled and anchors dragging.

An extremely interesting report later came back from another vessel which had been just on the edge of the main blast, and was driven south against the Gulf Stream and right over the Isthmus of Panama. Not only did this create the Panama Canal of such later great fame, but the vessel landed in the middle of a huge grove of berry-filled trees on the plateaus of Colombia. Upon draining the boilers to lighten the vessel and thus ease its return to sea, the hot steam that arose seemed to carry a remarkably aromatic and delightful odor; and as any boob-tube addict knows today, these lands became the world's greatest coffee plantations – thanks to Paul.

In later years Paul himself would tell many stories about his early camp life and friends – the sawyers, deckers, teamsters, roustabouts, swampers, skidders, road monkeys, river rats – and with great relish. A principal interest of his, of course, was what went on in the cookhouse. The cooks themselves were something else. For example, there was "Muttonhead" Mulligan, a big Irishman who invented the "Mulligan car" which ran the 'Jacks' lunches out to the pineries. He was also inventor of the famed "Mulligan stew", which made such a great hit in camp – until the loggers found out what he put in it, then rode him out of camp on a pole.

Norwegian cook "Cockroach Carlson" got his name from his strange attitude toward camp hygiene. "If you can't lick 'em, join 'em!" was Carlson's motto regarding the bug problem in his kitchen. So he not

Woodtick Wilson's self-flipping flapjacks.

12

only left it to the cockroaches to clean up his mess, but he deliberately fed the critters in an attempt to grow them so large he could use them to clean out the bunkhouse as well as the cookhouse. Carlson disappeared rather suddenly; and since there is no official report on his having left camp, the general conclusion is that the roaches finally turned on their sponsor.

"Woodtick" Wilson was Carlson's interesting successor – a real genius. This was the man who put popcorn in pancakes to get them to flip themselves. Ordinarily it would have been a great idea; but whenever the men got inordinately hungry, and Woodtick began making his cakes too fast, some came off the griddle before all the corn popped. The result was that it popped in the 'Jacks' stomachs. Now, nobody objects to a good hiccup now and then; but when a

big white blob comes out with it, and hits you in the eye, somebody has got to go.

Wilson's replacement in turn was "Wiener" Schnitzel, former leader of the German band whose instruments went to Paul, as earlier related. Wiener was of that stern Prussian type which brooks no nonsense; and when the odor of the lumberjacks' socks, which they aired out by stringing on a wire every night, began backing up into the kitchen even against his sauerkraut, he hit upon the diabolical scheme of cutting the toes off while the men were asleep. He figured that a "chimney effect" would improve the ventilation. But when the sleepy 'Jacks woke up to the 4:30 a.m. gong, they were unable to get dressed for lack of decision as to which end received the foot. What they did to Schnitzel is where we get the name "socks" today. They used to be called

"Wiener" Schnitzel invents the self-ventilating lumberjack sock to protect his sauerkraut from competition.

something else.

"Froglegs" Francois was the little Frenchman who took Schnitzel's place for awhile; and the cleverest thing that Froglegs did was to put green goggles on the oxen, then turn them out in the snow to graze midwinter. He saved the camp thousands of dollars on stored hay, and it's a wonder nobody had thought of it before.

Since rabbits were plentiful, and oxen were rapidly replacing the horses, Froglegs also saved the camp some money by making his famous "50/50 sausages" out of horse and rabbit – one horse and one rabbit. And these were *big*, just like Paul wanted them. Visitors usually thought they were logs coming into the cookhouse on skids, until some 'Jack stuck one of them with a fork and got squirted in the eye with fresh horse juice. Froglegs never did bother to clean

and dress an animal for cooking. "Zee flay-vor, she eez so *bon au naturel*", he would say.

Following Froglegs was the huge Polish cook "Poison" Ivitch. He came by his name quite honestly. In the first place, Poison used too much grease. One had to wear calked boots to keep from sliding out of the kitchen; and every gall bladder in camp was over-size, come Spring. Ivitch was also one of those Soup Nuts whose only kitchen utensils are kettles and dippers. Fish soup was his specialty; and he got his supply of fish by tossing a huge clod of chewing tobacco into the lake at sunset, then going out at dawn with a club and swatting the lunkers when they came up to spit. Once so many came up they couldn't get back down. These were the days when Bull Durham was first marketing it's D.R. or "delayed reaction" plugs. This meant you could stoke a wad before answering a

Happy Bull Durham days at Bunyan Camp 9.

14

call to the Walking Boss's office and not act quite like the slob you really are; and you could even bite off a quid before bunking down at night, then spit in the morning. Nobody ever found out what seasoning Poison used to give his soups such an unusual flavor, because nobody ever asked what happened to the toes his predecessor had cut off the 'Jacks' sox.

One cold day in November, when ice hadn't fully formed on the lake, the Tote Boss lost his whole team in a break-through while hauling dried beans from the village. When word came to "P.I." – as they soon came to call Poison Ivitch for short – that his whole winter's supply of beans had dropped into the lake, along with the ox team, he strangely enough seemed more excited than chagrined. Poland never had it so good. In less time than it takes to tell the story, Ivitch sent one team to dam up the outlet on the lake, and three others to haul all the slashings from the pinery down to the shore. Then he himself cut the harness on the floundering oxen to be sure they got into his recipe. After burning the slashings for three days and three nights, the camp had a whole lakeful of bean soup, complete with market-fresh oxtail. Some 'Jacks later froze the stew on sticks or ropes dipped into the lake, and brought them to the cutting camps to nibble on for afternoon snacks. Those who liked it hot drilled holes in their ax handles, filled them with soup, then kept it warm with their hands while chopping. This was the world's first thermos bottle.

Understandably, by the time "P.I." got through feeding Paul for a week or so, he had become trained to doing everything in a big way. He even learned how to make biscuits – real Polish Bunyan biscuits. They were so big and heavy that whenever he dropped one, it became a geological event registering on the Richter scale.

When P.I. later moved west, he brought many of the Bunyan camp legends with him – as well as creating a few more himself. After all, it takes a while to penetrate an inch of solid ivory; and he simply thought every camp had a Bunyan. His delight knew no bounds when he got to the Mississippi River and found that he could use the sternwheeler steamboats to stir his soups; and when he finally made it to the Weyerhaeuser camps on the West Coast, he celebrated the first dinner with such a vast "beanhole bean" cookout that to this day tourists misjudge the place as the crater of Mount Lassen.

Though never touching the stuff himself, Poison sure knew how to make home brew. In fact, his concoction was so powerful that no human being ever did drink it. Instead, trappers bought it by the barrel and put it out for bears. The first sloop was in most cases enough to make the animal turn inside out, leaving his hide for use as a sleeping bag. If by chance he managed a second sloop, everything dissolved – guts, bones, hide. Once a rabbit took a wee tiny taste of it, made three back-somersaults up a steep hill, then ran right up to a mountain lion and spit in his eye. Ivitch later became very mechanical-minded during the historic Industrial Age of modern civilization, proceeding to invent steam-driven potato mashers, force-fed helicopter batter stirrers, helium-cooled egg beaters, high-compression pancakes, nitrogenized decompression beans, and caisson soup bowls, among other things.

Just one shot of P.I.'s brew did it.

After Ivitch left Paul's camp, he was replaced by a couple enjoying only brief stays. The first was a hulking Russian, "Terror" Klosov, apparently a fugitive from some women's camp on the other side of the mountains. But he only knew how to cook borscht; and the warehouse soon ran out of beets, vinegar, vodka, horseradish and ginseng. His successor was the strange little Chinaman Wun Hung Lo from Inner Mongolia, whose name referred to the interesting fact that he was fully equipped with both jowls and eyebags, each of which hung low on the right side. It seems that this man had cooked for some camp built on the side of a hill, for he could only cook when facing west. They had to let him go because his cuts of beef were always slanted. Those who wanted it rare got some well done; those who wanted it well done got some rare; and those who wanted it medium could only enjoy the middle.

Of all the cooks in Paul's memory, the last and best was Sourdough Sam – so named because he made everything but coffee out of sourdough. Sam had only one arm and one leg, having lost the others when a barrel of his sourdough blew up.

Sam didn't start out too well. First, when he made his famous sourdough doughnuts, he had to call in Bellows Bologna to cut the holes with punch and sledge. Two men then ran a cedar pole through the hole and carried each one separately to the tables, on their shoulders. Some 'Jacks tried to eat them; but they lost all their teeth.

Second, when Sam made his first batch of his

famous sourdough pancakes, he got a drum of machine oil by mistake in place of molasses. At least nobody complained the rest of that month about their joints creaking. Even today the best cure for arthrytis is a machine-oil pancake.

With Sourdough's sourdough always rising all over the place, and in all the food, the men felt exceptionally well-fed because they were always bloated. The camp became the most popular one of its time. Everybody wanted to work there, and most of them did. The cook shanty finally got so large that men coming in for breakfast had to eat lunch if they sat at the wrong end. To keep the cookstove burning required clearing a whole "forty" each day just for firewood; and the draft finally got so tornadic that every time a flunkey put in a log, he went up the chimney with it. The crews also became immense, such that

they had one going out to cut, another on the way in, while the third was cutting. This made it necessary to cook breakfast, lunch, and dinner all at the same time. It was not enough to serve the donuts by rolling them down the floor from cookhouse to bunkhouse, the "taffles" serving tables also had to use roller skates, or they'd never make it before the food turned stone cold. And the loaves of bread ol' Sourdough turned out in those days were so large that the men chopped their way in, ate the insides only, then used the crusts for their bunks, or hitched them to camp horses for sleighs.

Just as all this was going along beautifully, Sourdough in his great hurry made the interesting mistake of grabbing a keg of blasting powder instead of baking powder for his pancakes – an event subsequently known sociologically, theologically, and

Sourdough Sam made everything – but *everything* – out of sourdough.

16

even geologically as *The Last Breakfast*. Not only the cakes rose, but the whole camp with it. Since nothing quite came back to where it was, the few survivors decided simply to start all over again.

For awhile it was touch-and-go for Sourdough's staying on the payroll. But lucky for him, the principal bosses who would have taken a very nasty attitude toward the whole thing never came back. Their own piggish nature was to blame. They were sitting as a group that fateful morning, at the end of the table nearest the kitchen so they could get their first "dibbies" on the stuff that went by, and while it was still hot. They had whistled down the taffles and grabbed triple orders as they roller-skated past. Now it so happened that the cakes didn't explode in the cookhouse – they just rose a few feet as the powder got ready. The final explosion came when the skaters dribbled a long line of fresh batter from the kitchen to the tables, as was usual for Sam's half-baked cakes when the 'Jacks got in too big a hurry to eat them. This then served as a fuse when the cookhouse end happened to drop into the fire. Sam himself, incidentally, escaped serious injury because he had taken a "nip" of some fermented syrup he always kept on hand to see him through the day; and he was lying face-down flat on the floor at the time, muttering: "I'll climb this wall if it takes all night!". The rest of the camp simply went up from where he was.

But dear old Sourdough Sam soon got back on the track by being the hero of the "Shot" Gunderson episode. Shot was the "Bull" Foreman of old Camp 8; and at the time now in question, shortly after reorganizing the camp, cutting was in the Skowhegan area. For some ridiculous reason that Shot himself

Yeah, Sourdough baked 'em big!

could never explain, he skidded his whole winter cut into the only lake for miles around which had neither inlet nor outlet. The situation was calamitous – but not for long, thanks to dear ole Sam. For Sam just mixed up a few team-loads of his famous sourdough and proceeded to dump it in the lake. When the stuff "riz", it simply carried the logs right up and over the hills into Kennebec River.

Flushed with this success, Sourdough went back to the pancake problem and decided to turn out a real winner, suited to the most homungous appetites. He got Bellows Bologna to make a skillet so big you couldn't see across it when the steam got thick. Advertising for men from the tropics who could stand the heat, he took the first six applicants, strapped hams to their feet, then taught them to play hockey on the griddle between each pour. The batter

he mixed in cement mixers, poured it with cranes and spouts, then ran the cakes out to the tables on conveyor belts. There wasn't a man in camp that year who could complain of being hungry.

Paul loved this big-time stuff, and soon became such fast friends with Sourdough Sam that he got the job of blowing the dinner horn – at least once. For not only did he blow a beautifully curved horn straight on the first blast, but he also blew down enough trees to spoil a whole stand of timber. So they begged him to blow *straight up* – not out. This he did; and there was no particular problem for an entire week. Then the place was deluged with telegrams pouring in from the U.S. Weather Bureau and every ship on the Seven Seas: "*PLEASE STOP whatever it is that you are doing!*" They couldn't figure out exactly what it was; but it seems that Paul knocked the

Paul blows the dinner horn. There's only one way to play it – COOL!

Paul goes to lunch with the 'jacks.

jetstream into a strange pretzel shape that was not only generating typhoons, monsoons, and so on, but was even getting them all mixed up into blizzoons, gabboons, and what have you.

Throughout the historic period of logging, there has always been the unwritten rule that nobody talks during mess. You do all your talking outside, and shut up when seated at the table. Like everything else in life, such an unusual custom had an unusual beginning. It began exactly here, and now, when Sourdough Sam was the cook, and Paul was still a young man in camp. And although nobody who was there at the time is still alive to tell about it, of course, so long as they were alive nobody ever forgot the event. It happened in this wise:

Paul was a polite boy; and one day when he crouched down and edged himself through the big log door on the bunkhouse, then pulled up a couple benches at the main table to seat himself, he turned around to say: "Thanks", to the several astonished 'Jacks who had fallen on the floor when he grabbed the benches. The draft blew out the cook's fire!

But cookee relit it; and after sufficient composure had been regained in the cook shanty, flunkies brought in the grub. Paul was so hungry he couldn't contain himself:

"PLEASE PASS THE GRAVY!!!"

This time he not only blew out the fire in the kitchen again, but there was more air coming out of these four words, of course, than out of the previous singleton; and while the flame went out temporarily, the coals became an emblazoned inferno, a

monstrous forge. By the time of the third exclamation mark, he had melted down the whole stove, exploded the sourdough loaves in the oven, and badly scalded all three of the slush cooks with evaporated soup before they could dive through the windows. Hissing white-hot streams of molten iron soon burned through the log walls and rolled sinuously down the hill, developing one of the strangest alloys ever known to metallurgists – iron from the stove, brass from kitchen utensils, copper and pewter from pots and ladles – all in turn carburized by the pants of the bull cook who was the last to dive out the window.

In fact, the building not only burned to the ground, but the fire was actually never put out. Sam's sourdough just kept it burning deeper and deeper until it finally sank into bedrock. Logging did eventually resume in that area; but 'Jacks down to the third generation had to be careful not to walk in their bare feet where the shack once stood because the ground was so hot.

And so it is that to this day every logging camp strictly observes that great and cardinal Cook's Rule: NO TALKING AT MEALTIME! Our boy Paul dunnit.

Next to cooking and eating, weather probably intrigued Paul the most; and often he would tell about the unusually hot summers and cold winters. One of the summers got so hot that corn stalks grew to 20 yards in height. Then she began to pop. And it kept popping until the ground was covered to a foot or more with stuff looking so much like snow that half the crew came back to camp with frostbite. Even several cows froze to death, though the thermometer showed +178°.

Mid-summer popcorn snowdrifts.

19

An even worse experience was the terrible winter when Paul was just turning 19. Not only did the thermometer freeze solid, and every maple tree explode into splinters from expansion of its frozen sap, but it finally got so bad that even the prices in the markets froze. Why, in the middle of February you could still buy a head of lettuce for ten cents. The only good thing about it was the tremendous supply of maple-sugar toothpicks from the exploded trees. The 'Jacks may not have eaten so well that winter, but at least nothing got lost in their teeth.

Even the fish went south; and when the Bull Cook tried to cheer the men with a huge pot of boiling coffee, it froze so fast they couldn't drink it because the ice was still hot. That cold spell broke every known record, the thermometer finally falling so low that it went around the bend and came back up to start melting.

But meantime snow and more snow! It got so deep nobody could tell where the forests were. The worst of it was that the men couldn't talk to one another because their words froze and fell on the ground, such that to this day they call it the Year of the Quiet Winter. When the spring thaw finally came, and the huge accumulation of lumberjack yack unfroze, the racket was so horrendous it was heard all the way to Paris.

Then it happened – and nobody will ever forget it – Paul's 21st birthday. At last he had become a *man*, and what a man!

To celebrate the fact that he need no longer worry about stunting his growth, Paul decided to take a pull of snuff just like the ol' 'Jacks. Putting a pinch to his nose, he began expanding his chest on the inhale. Three buttons exploded away from his jacket. Two of these lodged in the logs of the walls; but the third

Cold? Hell! Even their words froze!

20

passed out the window and not only downed a deer, but completely skinned it. When he finally leaned over backwards, then emitted that fatal **KAH CHOO-OOO!!!**, out went the coffer dam on the lake where the camp was booming its logs.

Unbeknownst, of course, to anyone in camp at the time was that the shock wave from that sneeze continued to travel west at the sonic speed of 1020 feet per second, heading directly for the Grand Cañyon of the Colorado. It was nothing but sheer fortunate circumstance that kept the men stunned and idle for some extended period of time, not knowing exactly what to do about what they had just witnessed; for in just a little short of six hours the echo returned from the west wall of the Grand Canyon and blew the dam back up. The Bunyan Stupor saved them from doing a lot of unnecessary work.

Those were the days when our Weather Bureau

was setting up its first stations in the Great West, pursuant to ideas of Jefferson and resolutions of Congress; and when the report of this action came in, there developed what became known as the famous Straight Line Mystery in the history of the U.S. Weather Bureau. To this day no meteorologist has been able to figure out why all trees and every living shrub from New England to the Grand Canyon of the Colorado River blew down flat in a westerly direction, then blew back up and back down again in an easterly direction, all in a single day.

One full century elapsed before an even greater mystery developed to intrigue and annoy the Space Age. We said that the dam blew back up; and this was so, except for the King Log. The 'Jacks had constructed this dam with three rows of huge upended logs, the second fitted to the crevices in the first, and the third in the crevices of the second, leaving a

Paul takes his first pinch o'snuff.

21

V-shaped opening at dead-center for the King Log – like the keystone in a Roman archway. When the dam went out, these logs all jammed in a downstream ravine of considerable narrowness, which accounts for the channeling of the return blast that subsequently set the dam back up. But apparently the thrust concentrating upon the King Log was simply too great. Searching proved useless. It could not be found, and finally had to be replaced by another.

Time rolled on; the Twentieth Century unfolded the mighty Apollo Mission; and then Neil Armstrong and his Apollo 11 crew touched down on the Moon, making that astonishing discovery which has so upset scientists debating the origin of our great satellite. For they simply cannot yet account for the presence of a huge log of white pine, measuring a full eighty feet in length and nearly five feet in diameter at the big end, driven at low angle for almost half its length into the crusty substance forming the surface of the Moon. The Moon is presumably a dead planet, and nobody ain't supposed to been there before us.

In the archives of the Weather Bureau at least six factual reports and explanations are still on file, delivered to the Bureau by descendants of witnesses who had been in the Bunyan camp at the time; and these have even been dug into by inquiring Apollo scientists, in hopes of relating the Straight Line Mystery to the Moon Pine Mystery and thus perhaps solving them both.

But there is something about the dignity of science which prefers a wrong explanation to an unnatural one. A two-way tornado of natural origins traveling 4000 miles from Maine to the Grand Canyon and back at a speed exceeding 700 miles per hour? A white pine that seeded itself by mistake on the Moon, from cosmic amino-acids? Well – at least there is a remote possibility that such a thing is remotely possible.

But a human sneeze? Complete with echo, yet? *NEVER!!!*

REFERENCE

1 . Brainard, Lucy Abigail: *The Genealogy of the Brainerd-Brainard Family in America 1649 - 1908*; Pub. by authoress at Hartford Press, Hartford, Conn., 3 vols. (1908); see entry 55: Ezra Brainerd

CHAPTER III

SOME NOTES ON WILD LIFE IN PAUL'S DAY

Not only Paul grew to huge and strange proportions in those far-off times; and it is of some interest to note the friends he made among certain rather weird animals, birds, fish, and even insects. We have already mentioned something about the cockroaches in camp. But let us now consider the bedbugs that also graced every logging outfit known to history. One crop that grew up in Paul's bunkhouse responded with more than ordinary enthusiasm to the new scale of action that seemed to fill the air with his arrival. For they soon reached such tremendous size they felt cramped in their old quarters, deliberately hiked off into the woods with the loggers' blankets, and became like wild bobcats except that they had more legs. So the 'Jacks naturally called them *wild bedcats.*

Somehow or other these bedcats succeeded in mating with the camp horses – interesting stuff – producing an 8-legged *bughorse* that ran so fast the men used them to move the spring thaw back to February. That is, when the cold north winds blew, the 'Jacks would scare the living hell out of a whole herd of bughorses with a charge of dynamite, whereupon the critters would outrun the north wind and make it blow south. At least that's what Einstein relativity tells us.

Eight-legged Bughorses moving the spring thaw back to February.

When other animals saw how much fun the wild bedcats and 8-legged bughorses were having, they quickly got themselves into the act of cross-mating also, until all Hades broke loose! Few youngsters ever had so many interesting creatures to wonder at and play with as young Paul. Consider the love affair of the antelope with a female jackrabbit, and the *jackelope* that shortly showed up as a huge rabbit with elk antlers! Some of these can still be found mounted on collectors' walls.

"Yeah, it's a **Jackelope**! – er, *was* a Jackelope!"

Then there was the biologically shocking occasion of the aggressive male skunk coming across a moose during rutting season. Obviously successful in his advances, he produced the awesome *skumoose* with its white-striped pelt, and sacs of potassium xanthate not only beneath the tail, but on the tips of its horns. In fact, this is where our slang expression *vamoose!* comes from, by way of the French. For *va* in French means "go"; and when the old French-Canadian 'Jacks north of Quebec first saw one of these animals – or rather first smelled one – they quite spontaneously designated and encapsulated the whole situation with the one brief expression *Va-moose!* When complete with exclamation mark this would not only advise one's companions to scram, but to get the cry-eye out of there, but quick! Ripley's *Believe It or Not* reported that loggers once unknowingly dropped a huge pine on a skumoose sleeping nearby in a thicket. Death was instantaneous, and so was the squeezing dry of every one of the sacs.

Now, where deer or elk are denominated by the number of "points" on their antlers, the skumoose gets his age and size statistics in terms of "sacs", since they add a new pair every year. This was a 16-er, a real beaut, with stuff hanging off him you wouldn't believe. You also wouldn't believe that the post-mortem stench was not only so thick you could cut it with a knife, but that for weeks the 'Jacks couldn't fell any more trees in that whole ¼-section. This was not because the odor was so bad – it was too thick to inhale anyway – but rather because the trees wouldn't fall. They just leaned into the stuff a bit and got stuck.

Weirdly enough, the famed *hodag* seems to have been half ox, half alligator, and half dinosaur – though nobody has been able to figure out how the dinosaur got there. These all presumably became extinct during the Cretaceous Period of the Mesozoic Era. One must have been left that even made it through the last Ice Age. Those who find the description of a hodag hard to swallow need only go to the remarkable Logging Museum in Rhinelander, Wisconsin, where the last known specimen is mounted for display. In fact, to this day all athletic teams at the Rhinelander High School are known as *The Hodags*. A study of materials found in the critter's stomach showed that its principal food was the porcupine. The hodags had apparently trained themselves always to swallow the porcupine head-first, then never to cough or vomit. It was strictly a one-way trip. The one mounted in Rhinelander either forgot, or got sick.

Hootpeckers, now long extinct, proved that this odd-ball and unprecedented promiscuity among

When a skunk mates with a moose,
the result is absolutely horrendous!

species lower than Man even extended to the birds in those early logging days. And here Mother Nature looked especially clever. For by crossing owls with woodpeckers, she produced a critter that did its pecking only at night, thereby handling those smart-alec tree worms that hide out when ordinary daytime woodpeckers come around.

Much more complex was the *triple-tailed bavalorous*; and Paul was particularly fond of this one. Seemingly half-buffalo and half-bird, with corkscrew horns, the "TTB" was even more remarkable for having three tails: The mid-tail served the usual purpose of tails, namely to protect private parts; an overslung up-tail was for flies that became too curious, swatting them before they ever got where they thought they were going to go; and finally there was a heavily padded underslung job to provide the bavalorous with a portable cushion for comfortable dining in a seated position. Nobody ever reported what this animal ate, because they were always too fascinated watching the other end. It is interesting to speculate that, in some ancient day, there was a certain amount of hanky-panky going on between sheep and goats in producing those upper two tails. For the sheep, we will recall, is the modest one in nature, always keeping its tail down; while the dam goat can't even get his down, and acts in general as though he were in the advertising business.

Hootpecker going after one of those
smart-alec night-worms.

One **Hodag** breakfast coming up?
NO! *Down* only! (Dam-m-n b'hoy!)

Triple-tailed Bavalorous, about to sit
on Tail III, swats fly with Tail II,
which was troubling his Tail I.

25

Perhaps the *splintercat* was part bird. Perhaps it was not. But it did seem to fly. With a head built like a mallet, this strange thing only appeared in early spring when maple trees were coming to life in the Indian "Sugar Bush". Striking a tree head-on from a terrific running or flying start, the splintercat would splinter the wood, then lick up the sap. Chief Hole-in-the-Day once reported that a particularly large one rammed his old Council Tree at the Sugar Bush on North Long Lake. But the critter had mistaken the elm for a maple and got stuck. They chopped him out, recovered the mallet, gave it to the Chief for use as a war club, then proceeded to chase the Sioux all the way out of northern Minnesota.

A close relative of the splintercat seems to have been the *axe-handle hound*. Though there were no indications it ever flew, the "AHH" had the same destructive nature toward wood, with a ravenous appetite for hardwood handles on axes, and on loggers' peaveys. We don't really have any idea what it looked like, since it only came out at night. But it was long a cardinal rule in a camp that loggers take their tools to bed with them.

Splintercat manufacturing toothpicks for Camp 9.

Completely feathered like a bird, though without other birdlike characteristics, was the ghastly and quite frightful creature called the *terrashot*. Paul only saw one of these – or rather its remains. It was built like a coffin, and of similar size, with eight wobbly legs. Parentage absolutely unknown. In fact, maybe it didn't have any.

Not until its thirteenth year did it come out of hiding, and only after producing its young – however it did that, if it did. In any event, on the night of the first full Moon, the matured terrashot would rush out on some lonely prairie, howl long and woefully thirteen times – then violently explode, become buried in its own crater, covered by its own debris. Paul once dug one up, but couldn't figure out how to put it back together.

The dread Terrashot comtemplates self-destruct.

27

Some birds of Paul's time were certainly birds, but also of unrecognizable parentage. Apparently some perfectly normal ones simply got infected with lumberjack enthusiasm and set out to try new and big things. Consider the *dingbat*, also called the *goofus* or *flu-fly bird*, which built its nest upside down to help its young to fly at any early age, and always flew backward so as to enjoy seeing where it had been. Naturally, it soon became extinct because it never saw where it was going. Legend has it that the old camp cook Froglegs Francois, who had a bird brain anyway, actually learned how to think like a dingbat. So he used to put his soup kettle where the critter was going.

Recipe of "Froglegs" Francois for his famous flu-fly-bird soup.

The *wild-blue-yonder-wonder* developed the novel feature of no legs, requiring it to remain in ceaseless flight. Necessarily feeding only on other birds, it mated but once in a Blue Moon, then flew so high its eggs hatched and the young learned to fly before hitting the ground. Paul dropped one of these once, along with a flock of geese, when using that special gun made by the camp blacksmith. But the men wouldn't eat it because there were no drumsticks.

As for the *mugwump*, this was really an ordinary bird, except for its peculiar habit of sitting astride a fence with its mug on one side and its wump on the other. It was easy to get a batch of these for supper, merely by using a club, and sneaking up on the wump side.

In the pineries among the lakes and hills, and all the way from Maine to the Upper Great Lakes and Mississippi Headwaters, there were three birds of quite remarkable characteristics. Consider the *tripodero heron*. As the name implies, this was basically a three-legged crane. But it had a barrel-shaped beak, which it used to stun its victims by shooting them with mud pellets. The third rearward leg steadied the bird against recoil. Paul didn't like to shoot these, lest they shoot back.

Tripodera Heron gunning down an afternoon snack.

In the neighboring hills was the *gilly-galoo*, distinguished by its building a rectangular nest right on the hilltop, then laying a clutch of square eggs so they wouldn't roll down. This bird was a real boon to loggers lost in the woods, because they always provided a square meal. —

Third among these special winged friends of Paul's was one closely related to the gilly-galoo. This was the *landslide-loup*, so named by the early French-Canadian voyageurs, their word *loup* for "wolf" referring to the horrible noise the critter made. For it also laid square eggs; but unlike the gilly-galoo, the landslide-loup not only hollered "OUCH!" when laying its eggs, but the racket sometimes became so horrendous as to trigger landslides.

Away from the lakes and hills, in the prairie country of the fearsome terrashot, there was an interesting birdlike creature called the *lassooper*. The modern roadrunner is its rather pitiful descendant, much reduced in size and minus its principal ornament. For the proboscis of the lassooper was a striking combination of the prehensile tail on a monkey and the trunk of an elephant. It was long and ropey, with a curlicue at the end which permitted it to lassoo rabbits.

A real sqaure meal of gilly-galoo eggs
comin' up and sunnyside up!

Lassooper lassooing its dinner.

Hence its name. Paul was often amused by its antics, but he thought it a bit gross.

Consider the *owl-eyed ripple-skimmer*. What in the world did such a thing have for parents? Fortunately, and remarkably enough, one specimen was captured and mounted before the species became extinct; and it actually remains today on display for skeptics in the Buckhorn Tavern at Rice Lake, Wisconsin. Its habitat was shallow bays where cattle would come to drink; for it fed almost exclusively on milk sucked from cows standing waist-deep in the water. Legend has it that, on breezy days when cows were loath to bathe because their udders got slapped by the waves, the OERS's would leap high out of water, drop into a low-angle glide against the wind, then skim off the ripples to restore a calm day. It is believed the species became extinct because of a fatal lack of ability to distinguish a cow from a bull.

About as difficult to catalog taxonomically, and far more dangerous to human beings, was the *toboggamonster* or *slide-rock bolter*, so called because of its principal habit. Apparently a marine mammal related to whales, the toboggamonster had a cavernous mouth, small evil eyes, and grab hooks for a tail. With these he would fasten himself to the top of a high rocky slope along the seashore, tail up, mouth down, awaiting his prey. His favorite dish was shell hunters and beachcombers, patrolling the shores with heads down in what Floridians call the Sanibel Crouch, and completely oblivious to everything else. Timed with the lifting of his tail, by some concealed and unknown ratchet mechanism, a tremendous drool of skid grease would pour from both corners of its mouth, to speed the toboggan-like descent, and to lubricate the passage of the victim or victims – some of them being known to swallow a whole hiking party in one gulp – from cavernous maw to abdominal bulkhead.

Yes, like any red-blooded American boy, Paul got a big kick out of his many interesting friends in woods, fields, rivers, hills, and lakes. The mugwump and jackelope he felt were a little blah, also the lassooper. He thought the hootpecker was pretty cute – until it whacked the camp's pickle barrel one night in search of vinegar maggots, and all the juice ran out. The gilly-galoo and landslipe-loup he loved because of their square eggs. Not only did they crisp up along the edges and at the corners while the yolks were still runny, but he could stack them and fry up ten dozen at a time instead of the usual two. The 'Jacks also boiled them and used them for dice.

Still other animals inhabited the wilds in those days; and we will try to round out the list so one can more fully appreciate the one Paul finally selected for a pet. Fortunately very rare was the *gumberoo*. For this animal closely resembled a huge bear, such that a hunter's natural instinct was to shoot it. BUT – the skin was so tough and elastic that the bullet would bounce right back and strike the hunter himself between the eyes. The only good thing about the gumberoo, as far as the lumbermen were concerned, was its explosively inflammable skin. If the animal ever got caught in a forest fire, it would explode and put the fire out.

Paul for a while became pretty much intrigued, and in some cases friendly, with the *hugag*, the *billdad*, and the *sqonk*. The first was a huge hybrid species of moose which was easily trapped on windy days, and of course served as an excellent camp food supply. Its lips were vastly overgrown, huge, and rubbery; and the hugag used these to wrap around trees, then pull them out of the ground so it could eat the roots. But on windy days the poor animal would become temporarily blinded by the flapping sail-like things blowing up over his eyes and getting hung up on his rack. At such times he was a sitting duck for any hunter.

As for the billdad, something somewhere somehow must have gotten genetically entangled with an Australian kangaroo, perhaps one that skipped ship where it served as a pet. A good guess is that it mated with a beaver out of shear frustration, and because of the somewhat lookalike tails. For this critter would sit on the shore of a lake, wait for a fish to jump, leap through the air with supersonic speed, stun the fish with the shockwave, then bat the miserable thing all the way back to shore with its tail, where it scaled it and ate it.

Paul made the horrible mistake of snagging a billdad on an otherwise beautiful July day. The camp cook went right ahead and boiled it up, having no idea that such a construction in nature might have rather unusual chemicals in its genes and hormones – such as might activate those strange molecules rather than destroy them when exposed to oven temperatures. At least the odor was delicious. For-

Adult Billdad goes fishin'.

tunately the first three men taking a bite reacted so suddenly and so strongly they probably saved the entire camp. For their bodies stiffened, their eyes glazed and rolled back under the lids, then – madly clutching the edge of the dining table to aid them in launch – they as of one man shot out the door and leapfrogged all the way into the neighboring lake.

So that was the last time for roast billdad. And to hell with the delicious odor.

Roast Billdad smelled so *good* – but, oh! the penalty!

30

Sad-eyed Sqonk dissolves in tears at
the sight of the Bull Cook.

Paul's friend the *Sinistrum wampus* or
Clockwise Wampus Cat.

Comes now the sqonk. Paul learned to love this animal, because its whole facial expression literally begged to be loved. Its puss seemed to have been designed by a thoughtful and loving Mother Nature, making it unusually large and remarkably flat to provide the perfect backdrop for its principal ornament – an immense pair of bags under eyes which constantly wept. Apparently the built-in eye-bag plumbing was so superb that the animal never had any need to urinate.

Because the sqonk was a night-feeding animal, when Paul first came upon one from behind, he was more attracted by the rather generous hams than by the face. So he lassooed it and brought it into camp. But when the sad-pan sqonk saw the Bull Cook coming at him with axe, butcher knife, and glint in eye, he sensed his villainous intent, and simply dissolved away in tears.

Paul also felt a certain amount of attachment for the *shagamaw* or *tote-road geezer*. One can only suppose that this strange evolutionary misfit of the northern pineries picked up genetic characteristics purely from environmental influences, hence in superb theoretical support of the otherwise highly discredited Russian biologist Lysenko. For although of obviously mixed bear and elk parentage, the shagamaw walked upright on its two hind legs like a man, and it would – or could – only travel in perfectly straight lines, either north/south or east/west. Occasionally one could be found splitting an angle at 45°. Furthermore, it always went an even 80 rods before changing direction; and when crossing proper-

ty that had been surveyed, it invariably stopped at section corners.

In fact, in one recorded case where a surveying team had been a little careless crossing the Rocky Mountains, next the Mississippi River while heading east, and the stakes were a bit off when reaching Maine, a shagamaw was seen stopping at a township corner, sniffing the air a few times, shaking his belly to balance the bubble level in his intestines – then disdainfully walking north 3 feet 6 inches and making the proper turn there. The shagamaw was easy to catch, because it could never get up much speed for reasons of having to make such sharp turns. The species finally drowned to extinction when, pressed farther and farther west by the advance of civilization, they tried to cross the Mississippi on section lines.

Some of the animals either bored Paul to death, or caused a feeling of revulsion. There was the *goatithro*, for example, which was also called *sidehill gouger* because of its peculiarity of long legs on one side and short on the other, to cut down the frustration in traveling along hillsides. However, whenever he tried turning around to go the other way, friend goatithro suffered frustration like you and I never knew. Small hills were easy, because he came back to where he was; but on things like river valleys, he had to just keep on going and going.

At such times and in such places, the poor thing earned the local name *wampus cat*, because it would simply sit down on its wampus for long periods of time and cry.

There were two kinds of wampus cats: Clockwise or *Sinistrum wampi*, and counterclockwise or *Dextrum wampi* – as one would judge their motions around a hill, looking down from an airplane. The clockwise cat, of course, had its short legs on the right; the counterclockwise cat, on the left. Paul thought the whole breed a bit gross.

Perfectly disgusting, in Paul's opinion at least, was the *whirliboopus*. This blood-thirsty creature, of very impressive proportions and sharply pointed rear hooves, would literally "hunt the hunter" and reverse the whole day's operation from fun to stark-staring tragedy. Where *whirliboopi* (Latin plural for *whirliboopus*) were plentiful, the rate of turnover in logging-camp personnel was really something. Scenting a hunter or logger coming down some trail, the whirliboopus would dig in his pointed rear hooves, then build up a spin of such furious measure that he became as invisible as a super-top. When the un-

suspecting victim walked into the tornadic vortex, he would literally explode into a bloody syrupy mass, which would hang in great dripping blobs and strings from all the surrounding trees. Whirliboopus would then come out of his spin and spend the rest of the day licking his dinner off the shrubbery.

Finally Paul got a bit stirred up over losing so many close friends, and then sorer'n hell when one got Swampy Bierhaus, the best swamper in camp. So he made it a point to accompany every crew working whirliboopus country. Walking in front, he would stop at the first sign of an updraft tugging at his shirt, spread his legs in a firm stand, then prepare to weather out the storm. The result was that the whirliboopus, at the other end of the spin, complete-ly unraveled. Thereafter no harm ever befell Paul's pals worse than getting slapped in the face with a wet whirliboopus gut. Occasionally two of the unraveled

That **dam** Agropelter!

32

whirliboopi would attempt to get back together again and mate; but nothing ever came of it, and the species soon became extinct.

Paul didn't like the *whintosser* either; and he shared the lumberjacks' general disgust for the *agropelter*. This last was a miserable ape-like creature which fed largely on hootpeckers caught during their daytime napping – which was bad enough, because the lumberjacks generally liked the hootpecker; but they added to this the nasty habit of pulling off dead branches and pelting the 'Jacks with them when they walked by.

As for the whintosser, he was something else. This seems to have been a special freak developed by some strictly Darwinian "survival of the fittest" process in early times of the terrible earthquakes at New Madrid near our later St. Louis. Some of them had migrated east.

Of general panther characteristics, the whintosser had the astonishing frame of a triangular box or prism, each of its three sides fitted with a full set of four legs. This made twelve legs in all, which explains the Latin name *Dodeca leggorum* given by taxonomists, who came upon some remains in an old logging camp. Eight of its legs were held in a curled position, ready for any earthquake which might suddenly flip him over, thus always leaving the carcass in a standing position come Hell or high water. Both neck and tail were swiveled; and the coarse hairs of its fur, also its toenails, slanted forward instead of backward – for reasons yet unknown. A simple way to trap the animal was to chase him into a big empty culvert, then pound it with heavy clubs on all sides at once. This made all twelve legs unfurl and go into action, whereupon the frightened animal got his directions mixed up, and usually tore himself apart trying to escape.

Disgusting earthquake-proof *Dodeca leggorum*.

Yes, in those days promiscuity was the going thing in the kingdoms of American wildlife. In fact, this is why we today refer to them as "wild life". It was *really* wild. Every male of every species simply shot right and left, with some receptive female usually standing by. It even exter.ded to the fish. Here are some of the critters we will only have time to mention, listed under the principal authors who described them. Everything else of theirs we have either swiped, or invented our own:

Cox[1]
roperite snaligaster
leprocaun
hyampom hug bear

Carson[2]
hinge-tailed bing-buffer
gowrow

LeSueur[3]
pinnacle grouse

Wyman[4]
redcats
engineer rat
hide-behind-hiatus
Vilas County tiger
pinnacle bird
milking trough

green-footed windpiper
gee-gee bird
Luebker eagle

Brown[5]
rumtifusel
luferlang

Edgar[6]
wild teakettle
bog hop

Stumpke[7]
rhinogrades or "snouter"
  or "snout leapers"
(*Phyllohopla bambola*)

Somebody named Ronald Searles has apparently also described a *humorless hyena* which made itself extinct by always seeking the last laugh.

REFERENCES

1. Cox, W. T.: *Fearsome Creatures of the Lumberwoods*, Press of Judd and Detweiler, Washington, D.C. (1910); reprinted in W. D. Wyman: *Mythical Creatures of the North Country*, pp. 25-65 (q.v.)
2. Carson, G.: *Fantastic Animals Prowl Tall Timber of Our Mythology*, Smithsonian **3**, 20-5 (Aug. 1972)
3. LeSueur, M.: *North Star Country*, Duell, Sloan and Pearce, New York, 327 pp (1945)
4. Wyman, W. D.: *Mythical Creatures of the North Country*, River Falls State Univ. Press, River Falls, Wisc., vi + 65 (1969)
5. Brown, C. E.: *Paul Bunyan and Tony Beaver Tales*, Pub. by author, Madison, Wisc., 18 pp (1930)
6. Edgar, M.: *Imaginary Animals of Northern Minnesota*, Minn. Hist. **21**, 353-6 (1940)
7. Stumpke, H.: *The Snouters: Form and Life of the Rhinogrades*, Univ. of Chicago Press, Chicago, IL., 92 pp (1981)

CHAPTER IV

PAUL GETS A PET: BABE THE BLUE OX

At one time Paul thought he would like to trap and tame a deep-winter snow wasset or *Mustelinopsis subitiverax*, as some half-educated under-cerebrated boob from Yale named him. (The present author got his doctorate from Harvard.) But this strange weasle-like monster shed its legs each winter so it could slither serpentlike beneath the snow. While it was easy to spot when sticking its head out of the drifts, one could never tell whether it was going or coming; and this made it almost impossible to know where to set your trap. His thick white fur, however, was specially attractive because there were no leg holes, making the pelt ideal for a sleeping bag. Larger ones could be split down the middle to provide a fine pair of mattresses.

Paul also gave some thought to taming a *wapaloosie*, sometimes called a wallapaloosie by those of sloppy diction. This was a small sausage-shaped animal resembling a dachshund, with rabbit ears, spiked tail, and feet like a cat for climbing trees to get its favorite mushrooms. But the lumberjacks used the nice warm fur for mittens; and it always repulsed Paul to see the 'Jacks take their gloves off, and have the things start crawling up the axehandles.

THEN ONE FINE DAY in the middle of May, Paul struck oil: A BLUE OX! Logger legend has never been the same since. Here is the gist of this superhistoric event:

Paul was out by himself on a camping trip at the time; and he had pitched on the shores of Mooselookmeguntic Lake – and if anyone thinks we are straying from hard facts and cold geography in this narrative, go look up these dam places yourself on any good map of Maine! There were four principal logging areas in those days: One on New Brunswick's Gaspé Peninsula near Restigouche and Dalhousie at the mouth of the Matepedia River; a second in the general area of Chemquasabamticook Lake at the head of the Allagash; a third near Lakes Caucomgomoc, Umbagog, and Mooselookmeguntic, all of which are drained by the Androscoggin; and the main one – which gave the State of Maine its misspelled name – on the headwaters of the Penobscot. This last had two principal tributary systems, the lake chain from the northwest near Mt. Katahdin running Chesuncook → Millenocket → Pemadumcook, while that from the northeast began with Lake Magagundavic and the Chiputneticook chain. The large watersheds of the St. Johns, Kennebec, and Miramichi had already been logged.

So here was Paul on the heavily wooded shores of beautiful Lake Mooselookmeguntic, in days when its virgin timber was yet uncut. This was the late closing stage of the famous Winter of the Blue Snow. Ice on the lake was at least eight feet thick, and some of the blue stuff was still falling. Suddenly Paul heard a most tremendous commotion out on the lake. Apparently the ice out there was shattering, and a huge hole developing. Something most unusual was certainly attempting to emerge from the frigid waters. But what? A lost walrus? A polar bear? The famed Sasquatch? E.T.?

No! A huge rack of bull horns immediately knocked out all those assumptions. Then came an enormous head, shoulders, hocks, hooves, belly, belly button, buttocks, hams, more hocks, more hooves, tail – AN OX!?

A newborn *baby ox*? At such a size? And all of it *pure blue*!? Even the horns and the belly button!?

Everything about the critter was normal for a baby ox except its size, color, and the fact that it came up out of a frozen lake. At first Paul thought the blue color resulted from the dumkat snow, which made everything blue that winter. But this yammuck was still blue after he shook the snow off. Then Paul thought perhaps he was blue with cold; but not so. He stayed blue even after he warmed up.

Paul could scarcely believe what he was seeing, nor has anybody else ever since. For "Babe" was, is, and forever will be, not only one of its kind, but the only one kind of all kinds. Wherever a bunch of liars are gathered together, there Babe will be found, and there only. He became the perfect foil – oops! pal – for Paul. Both of them utterly outside both reason and sanity.

But then Mooselookmeguntic has long been famous for coming up with a lot of strange things besides its name. Is not this the home of the owl-eyed

Historic arrival of Babe of Blue Ox through the ice of Lake Mooselookmeguntic during the Winter of the Blue Snow.

ripple-skimmer, the fur-bearing smallmouth bass, and the diamond-studded crab? The daisy-picking muskellonge, cross-eyed walleye pike, the cigarette whitefish that smokes itself? Can one forget the northern pike here that went south for the winter? The all-time record lunker that swallowed some fisherman named Jonah and even got written up in the Bible?

Measuring a full five axehandles across the horns, and hanging at perhaps two tons, this blue mother-less orphan soon showed himself as strong as the breath of a Tote Boss. For he had clambered easily up on the ice. Nor was there any trouble getting him to the campsite on shore. He came right over to Paul, like like seeking like, and nuzzled the big young log-ger a real wet ox nuzzle. So Paul warmed him in front of his campfire, then folded his tent and began hiking his new "little" friend back to Camp. Not very "little" to us; but to Paul he was "Babe" at first sight, and till death do us part.

Fortunately it was only a few miles; for every time Paul looked back, the critter was another two feet taller. The team boss made the mistake of letting Paul put him in the camp barn for the night; and next morning the barn was gone. Paul soon found it, however, by following the tracks into the hardwood forest on the neighboring forty, where the rather unusual beast was munching on oak trees with the barn stuck on his back.

They were a natural pair, love at first sight.

36

The ever-obliging Babe airing out the Sunday wash.

BABE THE BLUE OX was the name he soon got by general consent – Babe for the genus, and Blue Ox or *Glaucus oxyrhincus* for the species. Babe was docile by nature; and he quickly came to love Paul, as Paul came to love him. It was love at first sight, and a natural pair, at least from standpoints of size. Where Paul had cleaned out a whole mess hall before the camp geared up to his appetite, thirty or forty bales of hay including the wire scarcely made a between-meal snack for Babe. It took six men with peaveys to get the wire out of his teeth after each meal – until they discovered they could dissolve it out with camp coffee.

Babe soon won the hearts of all the other lumberjacks as well. He could pull anything just so it had two ends, or one end and one beginning. He quickly took up Paul's old job of pulling the logging roads

straight; and it was really something when Paul found he could hitch Babe to a whole section of 640 acres, drag it to the boom landing where the sawyers would clear it off, then have his little pal drag it back to where he got it. Running six such trips a day for six days a week covered an entire township; and the reason that there has never been any Section 37 on land surveys is that Babe was very religious. He absolutely refused to work on Sunday. But his nature was also considerate and accommodating. So he split the difference with his lumberjack friends, hauled an extra load late Saturday night, and then left these late Saturday sections at the landing to wash away in the spring rains. He further solicited their friendship by spending Sunday in meditation outside the bunkhouse so the men could string wires across his horns and hang out their wash. But never again during

Christmas. For Babe's vibes once got so high he went completely over into 4-D and forgot to bring their clothes back.

Nothing on this mundane sphere is ever perfect, and Babe presented a couple problems. First, having had a cold-water birth, he would only work when snow was on the ground. But the 'Jacks solved this by whitewashing the logging roads during summer months to keep him on the job.

Second, his upkeep was understandably a bit of a problem. When thirsty, Babe could only drink downstream of any logging operation because he would dry up the river. But even this was turned into a good thing. For on one of the big spring drives, Chris Crosshaul made the gustofallous mistake of running the wrong logs all the way to Penobscot Bay. At that time they were logging the chain of lakes running from Chesuncook to Millinocket and Pemadumcook at the base of Mount Katahdin. (Ha-a-a? You don't believe it? Go look at your map!) These drain into the Penobscot River at Mattawamkeag, which runs past Bangor into Penobscot Bay.

Now, one simply cannot run a boom upstream. But Paul took Babe over to Lake Pemadumcook and gave him an overdose of salt cake. The result was that Babe drank the Penobscot dry so fast that its flow reversed and all the logs came back. But it was tough on the freshwater fish until the salt water backing up from Penobscot Bay got rinsed out.

Shoeing Babe was a job in itself. First they had to

Big Ole sank knee-deep in solid rock carrying one of Babe's shoes from forge to hoof.

On the return trip, he'll haul the cellars.

log off New Hampshire just to make a place for him to lie down; and for each shoe, the crew had to go west to Michigan to open a new mine on the Gogebic or Marquette Iron Ranges. It took Bellows Bologna seven days and seven nights just to fire up his forge for one shoe; and each was so heavy that, when Big Ole went to carry it to where Babe was patiently waiting, he sank knee-deep in solid rock.

With his brand new shoes, however, Babe got plenty handy on his feet. Crazy Jim the bullwhacker helped him develop terrific speed by tying a bright orange sash around his middle and entering him in the St. Patrick's Day parade. The footprints he made were so far apart that only Paul could track the animal, since he was the only one who could see the next print without climbing a tree. They were also so deep that it was necessary to use mining equipment to save anybody who fell in. Once a whole pioneer family – man, wife, and 2-year old baby son – simply disappeared; and it was not until the son was 40 years of age that he was finally able to climb out and report the accident.

When it became necessary to move camp, the loggers didn't have to rebuild their quarters any more, as in the old days. They simply harnessed Babe to one building at a time, had him pull it to the new campsite, then go back and pull over the cellars. This was hard work, of course, causing Babe to develop an especially enormous appetite; and once he swallowed the whole cookstove in his hurry to get at his meal. The thing was red hot, and it started a peat fire in his lower bowel. This made a very impressive sight to see Babe walk by on that cold morning, since an ox usually steams only at one end. In fact, the unusual event gave "Shot" Gunderson his nickname – the famous logger we earlier mentioned in relating the Sourdough Episode. For Gunderson, like most of the tough 'Jacks, had seen enough mad bulls to learn how to stand his ground, glare back at it eye to eye, and even take a few snorts himself – if such were available. But when Babe came by that cold and steamy morning, snorting at Gunderson from both ends, that dear and formerly brave man suddenly got in such a great hurry that he didn't even bother to run. He simply *shot* right up the nearest tree.

Our word *asphyxiation*, incidentally, comes from those days, when it used to be spelled with a double "s". Indeed, Babe's condition caused some serious problems in camp, and wherever else there wasn't an awful lot of fresh air.

Funny thing – speaking of horrendous, homungous, and even hohomungous odors: For awhile the loggers thought it was the bull-whacker Bill McGill. So they called him Brimstone; and the name stuck even after they found out that it was Babe. Brimstone took a great liking to Babe, and soon got to know him so well you'd think he had ridden through him on a bale of hay, holding a lantern. Babe actually didn't know left from right; and it would be easier to get a mule to respond to "giddap!". BUT he did know what "chow!" meant, even if you said it in a whisper, and in Afghanistanese.

So Brimstone Bill McGill came up with one of the greatest programming scenarios in the history of education, the result of a fantastic discovery. For all he had to do was get Babe in some position where his

Babe's Moon landing, 13 November 1833.

feed was to his left, holler "CHOW!" to get him in immediate launch position, then fix the navigation with a loud "GEE!". Soon he had Babe intensely responsive to every command that is useful between man and beast:

"CHOW! GEE!" . . . go right
"CHOW! HAW!" . . . go left
"CHOW! MUSH!" . . . straight ahead

He didn't need the "giddap", because the "chow" did that. So he made Babe sleigh-responsive by borrowing the huskies' commands.

Unfortunately, however, Brimstone had the serious personal problem of developing terrible hiccoughing at the time of the full moon. On the night of 13 November 1833 – and Indians as well as astronomers have ever after kept the event carefully inscribed in either memory or written record – Brimstone went out to the barn to give Babe his usual midnight snack of three tons of potato peels set aside for that purpose by the bull cook. The moon was full, and Brimstone was in his usual form. He simply could not get out one word without a loud hiccup. So when he hollered:

"CHOW! 'UP!"

that's exactly where Babe went – straight up. He scooped the Apollo Missions by 137 years. He was not only the first terrestrial on the Moon, but to this day retains the distinctive record of being the first and *only* Blue Ox.

Crater Archimedes records his lunar landing site, and the Great Meteor Shower of 13 November 1933 records the splash. Nobody knows exactly how Babe got back, except we know he did.

Babe gets bewildered by the crosseyed-cockeyed fly.

Babe was also directly responsible for one of Paul's greatest inventions. We will recall that the 'Jacks used to string a wire across his horns for hanging out their laundry. What they didn't know was that Babe could wiggle his horns much like a rabbit wiggles its ears; and one fine summer day when a fly sat on his nose, there was real trouble in camp. It was Sunday, and the wash for the whole week was hung out.

Up to that time Babe had very graciously wiggled his horns in the same direction – both either to the right or to the left – such that the only effect was to dry out the clothes quicker on account of the increased draft.

But on the particular day in question, the fly that sat on Babe's nose was cross-eyed. Worse, as Babe gazed upon it with his usual bovine contentment, he was shocked to observe that the fly switched back and forth from being cross-eyed to being cockeyed. This is not customary for flies; and it got the gentle animal so confused that, when he twitched his horns to scare the fly off by shaking the laundry, he did what the fly did – first shook them cross-eyed, then cockeyed. When the slack came out of the line from going from the one to the other, it did so with such terrific force that the wire snapped and sent the laundry flying far out in the woods, such that most of it was never recovered.

Now, it was bad enough for the men to have to work naked in Mosquito Country until they got new clothes; but the real problem developed later when they got the clothes, stunk 'em up as usual during a week of hard work, washed them on Sunday morning – then had no place to hang them up to dry. In the first place, they simply could not trust Babe so long as cross-eyed flies were around. In the second place, their wire was gone with their clothes, so it would do no good even if they trusted him in the first place.

Meantime Paul had been experimenting with spiders and spiderwebs, getting a particularly fine specimen in the bunkhouse to grow so large he could finally mate it with a horse and develop a horseweb instead of a spiderweb. The men had already been using some of this for rope. However, the *spidorse* finally died for lack of flies big enough to keep him fed properly. So what else do you feed a spidorse?

At that time there was a new Bull Cook in the camp, an Indian named Pogamoggan. This man combined two remarkable qualities: First, his eyesight was keener than that of a hawk; second, he was the lousiest janitor that the Camp had ever known. There were cobwebs developing in the bunkhouse that finally grew so large the men were using them for fishnets. In fact, this was the Camp that developed the "muzzle loader" bunk, requiring end-loading, because the cobwebs running the length of the bunkhouse made it impossible to get in or out from the sides. The men even had to be careful how they answered the morning wake-up gong, lest they forget themselves and jump out of their bunk into the cobwebs.

Nevertheless, none of the strands seemed tough enough nor long enough to replace the lost wire and serve as a laundry line on Babe's horns, even if they got rid of the cross-eyed flies. Plainly, what was needed was an upgraded cob, much as Paul had upgraded his pet spider. The question was: *Where is the cob that makes the cobweb?*

Since he had never been able to find one himself, Paul called in Bull Cook Pogamoggan, who immediately went to work searching with his keen eyes. In no time at all, he not only came up with a perfectly gorgeous specimen, but even with a matched pair! It essentially opened a new chapter in the science of entomology.

In less time than it takes to tell this strange story, Paul and Old Pog had the two cobs mated, then fed their kids with the dust and gunk that only a sloppy Bull Cook like Pogamoggan could supply. They grew to perfectly horrendous size – except that nobody but Pogamoggan could see them.

Finally the great day arrived, and they stretched a gorgeous cobweb across Babe's horns. Then they hung up the camp laundry. It was a terrific layout. The 'Jacks purred like cats. Pog could have been elected President.

But shortly things got completely out of hand. The

Paul's pet Spidorse spinning camp rope.

Historic photograph of old Pogamoggan's matched pair of cobs on their wedding day.

honeymoon was over. For the mating instincts of the cob are beyond all description. There were literally clouds of little cobs growing up all over the place; no 'Jack even dared go to sleep anymore, tired as he was, because he wasn't able to snore. How can a lumberjack sleep without snoring? Yet, as soon as a mouth opened anywhere in that bunkhouse, every tooth in the man's head got strung with cobwebs 'til he nearly choked to death. The situation became unbearable. The cobs had to go. And although they were smart little cobs, rapidly maturing, nobody was going to wait for them to go away to college.

Since Bull Cook Pogamoggan was the only man with eyes keen enough to see 'em, they gave him the camp rifle and told him to go to work. So Old Pog pulled up a stump to make himself comfortable, sat by the door to the bunkhouse, and every time a cob went by he shot it dead. Some of the big ones, it is said, splattered all over the door, though nobody but Pogamoggan, of course, could see the mess. Within about six months he had killed them all, and hauled the corpses out in the woods. As one can readily understand, instead of piling their little bodies higher and higher to make a heap, because of the cobs' invisibility he had to pile them deeper and deeper to make a hole.

And to this day, the strange pit in Section 11 of Township 135 west, Range 29 north, 3rd Principal Meridian, remains to mark the famous Cob Cemetery outside Paul Bunyan's Camp Nine.

Pit of piled down bodies of deceased invisible cobs.

CHAPTER V

PAUL BECOMES A LUMBERJACK

When Paul celebrated his 21st Birthday – we will recall the snuff incident – all the camp naturally celebrated with him. For he was now a *man*, and could be put to work.

And what a man! His very footprints gave rise to all later legends of Big Foot and Sasquatch[1], also the *Taku he* of the Lakota Sioux, the *Omah* of the Huppa Indians, *Dzoonokwa* of the Bella Bella and Kwakiutl, the *Bukwus* of the Tsimshian[2], *Naba-Cha* or "Big Man" of the Dogrib Indians in Northwestern Canada[3], *Wisakedjak* of the Cree, *Napi* of the Blackfeet, *Gloscap* of the Micmacs and Malecites in New Brunswick, the Champlain Monster[4], the mysterious *Tsawhawbitts* of the far Southwest[5], probably the Canadian sea monster *Ogopogo*[6] – and possibly even the *Mokele-Mbembe* of African tribes[7].

Just to mount his birthday cake, a special grandstand had to be constructed; and six shifts of cooks from neighboring camps joined together to bake his cake. The day almost ended in disaster, however. For

Paul's 21st birthday cataclysm – er, celebration.

Paul's 4-bit rotatory axe.

Speaking of spindles: Babe himself once got into this kind of act, and similarly came up with an invention that has been a boon to loggers and farmers ever since. Spring always brought out the horse flies; and some of these were not only enormous, but in Maine their stingers carry pure sulfuric acid rather than the usual formic acid. When they bit Babe on his hind end, it made him howling mad. It was not enough to keep brushing them off with his tail – he wanted to swat them so hard they'd not only never forget, but would be unable to remember never to forget, or anything else. Hopefully it would even carry the message through their genes and chromosomes unto the third and fourth generation.

So Babe began doing tail calesthenics by wrapping the appendage around some sturdy oak, then rocking it back and forth. But these flies were also pretty smart: They would wait till the tail was thus engaged during Calisthenics Hour, then lace into poor Babe's exposed butt.

And so it was that at high noon on the third Tuesday of the hottest July of record, grandad fly ran his 3-inch ovipositor into a very juicy and tender spot, injected about a half-liter of smoking 98-degree Baumé H_2SO_4, and prepared to siphon off his reward. Babe simply couldn't wait to unwind his tail into swat position. So the tree had to do the unwinding. Roots snapped off several feet from the trunk; the tree went into spin like a dust-devil on the Wyoming deserts; dirt and rocks flew all over the State of Maine; and down dropped the tree into its own post-hole. The fly went with it, which pleased Babe no end – the front end, that is; and the whole camp was pleased because Babe had invented the post-hole digger. This later became the famed Rotary

when Paul blew out the candles, half the camp was leveled by the blast; and all that hot air brought on an early spring thaw that sent the whole winter's cut downriver before they had time to barkmark the logs and pull them into booms. Fortunately nobody was seriously hurt, though it took several days for the stunned men to find their way back out of the woods.

Mixed emotions attended Paul's entry as an adult member of the Camp staff. Everything he did was huge – monstrous advantages and horrendous disadvantages. Even the lice in his clothes seemed to catch the "big" fever; and on Saturday nights or Sunday mornings, when the crews all gathered to "bile out the lice" in the great camp tubs, a special group had to be assigned to stand alongside Paul's clothing with baseball bats and knock down the big ones when they tried to climb out.

Paul's first job in the woods was that of an axeman – and his amazing deeds are memorialized today by that elite group in the Brainerd, Minnesota, Rotary Club known as *The Paul Bunyan Axemen*. Paul began with the usual single-blade of the neophyte, but graduated quickly to the double-bit so he could cut on both the front and back swings. Even this was too slow for him, so he got Bellows Bologna to make a four-bit axe in propeller arrangement. He then did his cutting by spinning the handle between his hands much as Indians use a spindle for fire by friction. Trees began flying everywhere – whether the Walking Boss wanted them there or not.

In fact, they wouldn't let Paul use an ordinary axe, because on his first swing he would drive it into the wood so far up the handle that it would take the rest of the crew half a day to drop the tree and get his axe back out.

Babe invents the post-hole digger – thanks to a dam fly with H_2SO_4 in its proboscis.

44

Yeah, the regular crew next week will log the valleys.

Well Driller used by the legendary Kemp Morgan in America's Wild West.

In those days the 'Jacks used to sharpen their axes by going to the top of a hill and digging loose a big boulder. As it rolled down the slope, they would run alongside. Paul thought this rather stupid, and shortly invented the grindstone. His first model had to be toned down somewhat, however. For it was so big that the Chore Boy, little Ankelosis Anderson, had problems turning it. Once around, and it was pay day.

Paul also took his hand as a sawyer. This proved fine during the partner pull; but when it was Paul's turn to pull, his partner simply took off over the trees and out into the wild blue yonder.

So Paul invented his own saw, with a spring on the partner end to take up the slack and give the man chance to lash himself to a tree. The trouble was that the saw was so long it could only cut trees off the tops of hills, requiring a total reorganization of camp crews so that others could fell those in the valley. Paul's classic remark to his partner has ever since been a part of logging history:

"I don't care if you ride the saw, but please don't drag your feet!"

Obviously things were not working out too smoothly with Paul in the woods. He tried to be helpful by running his own cutting crew on three 10-hour shifts per day; but for this, of course, he needed night lights. So he invented the *Aurora*

borealis. This then brought up a new problem of having to pay his men undertime instead of overtime, since the 24-hour day fell six hours short of his workday. One of Paul's better contributions to the logging industry, before they kicked him out of the woods, was the famed *canthook.* Its invention came about in this wise: Paul kept hearing men complain that they *can't* move this huge log, or *can't* do that. So he simply invented a canthook which can, and went ahead and did it.

Nevertheless, Paul himself soon agreed that he was not cut out for work with cutting crews – with him there, nobody else was needed. But this would put a lot of men out of work. So he offered to go back and help in the cookhouse. The result of that disastrous move became what is known throughout logging history as *The Year of the Great Empty Plate.* With every man in the place, except Paul, already mere skin and bones by the middle of January, they rapidly demoted him from Cookee to Flunky to Bull Cook.

As Bull Cook in this particular camp, it was Paul's job to blow the horn calling the men to chow – even though there was nothing left to eat at the time. At first they gave him a steer horn; but when he blew it, all of the cattle on adjoining farms, including those belonging to the Camp itself, sickened and died. They thought it was the Four Horsemen of the Apocalypse signaling the end of the world; and that was a sickening thought.

When Paul pulls *down*, everything else goes *up*!

So they got him a huge tuba. Naturally, the first note straightened it out, making a tube out of the tuba.

In fact, everything Paul blew straightened out. Fortunately for musical posterity, the French were far across the Atlantic Ocean; and it was only through those dear segregated people that the French horn has been preserved in its original unstraightened form. The peasants in the valley of the Alps, however, thought the racket they heard coming all the way across the Atlantic rather pleasing – probably because of dilution while crossing the ocean; and to this day they use Paul's invention of the straightened-out Alpine horn.

Purely in desperation, Camp Foreman Bull Whiskers put Paul on the road-icer. This was a team-drawn water tank with a loading barrel, which the crew would run out on some convenient lake or river. There they would cut a hole in the ice and load the tank. During a night shift, when all crews were back in the bunkhouse, they would then travel the tote roads and skidways while dumping the water to form ice, the teamster calling the shots as to when to pull the bungs. This special wagon had a dunk-side and a haul-side, the bucket or barrel being lowered into the hole on the former, and hauled to the tophole by an over-top rope pulled from the latter.

Unfortunately, when they started Paul on the dunk side, the hole he cut was so big the team fell in.

Much worse, however, was the mess they got into when they changed him to the haul side. For his mighty yank not only ran the bucket up the slide, but over the top and far out into the distant woods – before his two helpers had chance to let go the bail.

Two days later they found them stuck in the top of a big pine about eleven miles away, dazed but still bravely hanging on to the precious bucket.

This embarrassed Paul so much that he decided to go it alone, to avoid further maiming of his assistants. For this he built his own road-icer, and hitched it to Babe the Blue Ox. The Camp by this time had made so many moves it was now up in Labrador. At least that had the advantage of giving him the whole Hudson Bay for dunking, avoiding the problem of draining a lake every time he loaded up.

So in his own big way, then, Paul proceeded to pull water from Hudson Bay, which conveniently refilled itself by torrential flows of incoming water through Hudson Strait, Davis Strait, Baffin Bay, and from both the Atlantic and Arctic Oceans. This put the *ebb* tide in the great neap tides of the Bay of Fundy, which were still running since his baptism.

More disastrous, however, was the result of Paul's road-icing. For this over-size ministration not only ic-

The famous Johnny Inkslinger.

ed the tote roads and skidways, but soon piled the ice so high the roads became great glaciers. When the ice finally flowed under its own weight, glaciers proceeded to cover all of Eastern Canada, then went on to plow up the neighboring states from Maine west to the Dakotas. Geologists have always been puzzled as to why where was a fourth Great Ice Age called the Wisconsin, when all calculations show there should only have been three – Nebraskan, Kansan, and Illinoian in that order. Little wonder; for the first three were Acts of Nature, but the fourth was an act of Paul Bunyan with his faithful Babe the Blue Ox.

After the ice melted and the glaciers receded, all the surviving loggers, who had fled to Florida to escape Paul's Ice Age, regathered and set up a new camp. This time they decided that the only thing to do with Paul was to give him a desk job, thereby keeping him completely out of the woods as well as out of the cookhouse. In those days there was a funny little bookworm 'Jack amongst them called Johnny Inkslinger. Johnny wasn't worth a dam on a cutting crew, but he was sure something on books. He carried so many pencils behind each ear you would swear he was wearing a wig. Then he had

three in each hand so he could do six-column bookkeeping all at once, using three to add or multiply, the other three to divide or subtract. Johnny always carried an eraser clipped to the end of his nose; and he used the waxed points of his curved mustache to hang invoices and memos.

So they got Johnny and Paul together, and built a special desk looking something like a roofed drydock used for an ocean liner. They put Paul at one end to do the writing, and Johnny at the other to do the figuring. For entries in ink, they ran two hoses from hydrants, one for Paul's left hand and one for his right, while still a third was standing by filled with red ink.

With Johnny and Paul working together, the bookkeeping went pretty well. Paul contributed the invention of using his hutch of cottontail rabbits for blotters. He simply stuck a stick in front of his shirt, and another in the back, with a carrot hanging on a string off each end; whereupon the rabbits kept running around him in circles while he laid down the wet ink.

Johnny's greatest contribution was probably the slitting of his pens and pencils to invent double en-

47

Paul's sox were something else –

tries. This doubled what the 'Jacks owed for their socks, tobacco, mackinaws and other things bought from the PX, such that the Camp was soon making more from his bookkeeping than they were from selling logs. The principal problem was to keep the Camp from ever going into the red, even for 5¢. Once this did happen; and before the valve on the hydrant could be switched back to black, the company went in debt $3 million. But Johnny soon balanced out that deficit through saving ink by not dotting his i's or crossing his t's.

Both of these geniuses deserve credit for what happened when a peddler visited the Camp one day selling watches. Naturally, he was charging the biggest prices for those that kept the best time. But while he was tapping other 'Jacks for sizable wads, Paul whispered something to Johnny, who made a few quick calculations. They then bought the lousiest and cheapest watch that the peddler had; and it ran so fast that it paid for itself in the first week. Even the 'Jacks learned to love that timepiece because every fifth day they got two breakfasts; also, when some boring Sky Pilot would drop in, filled with sermons for Sunday on the perfectly disgusting topic of how to be good boys when having a night out on the town, for them it was Tuesday and they had already had

their night out on the town.

While this desk job proved to be a good deal for a while, an entirely different and unexpected kind of problem eventually arose which ended Paul's days for any kind of sedentary life. Such prolonged inaction, with constant sitting at a desk, made his feet perspire something frightful, with no satisfactory way to air them out. Even by the end of the first week their office was cited by OSHA. On the third day of the second week, Johnny passed out from the air pollution, upsetting ink that spoiled a full day's records; and by the fourth day, the rising fumes actually lifted Paul's whole end of the table, spilling ink and wrecking half their books. It was in that camp, and at that time, that the movement originated which finally consummated centuries later in the E.P.A. It was also the incident that later gave the Montgolfier brothers their idea for the world's first hot-air balloon.

So by common consent of all parties concerned, and the violent urging of some, Paul was through in that office, or any office. Principally to clean out his feet, they gave him a job as a "river pig", riding the great slippery logs during drives down the Kennebec. Paul became a real "white-water buckeroo". He rode water that was so rough other men were even afraid to drink it. He could spin a log so fast that the bark came off and the bare log rolled up the bank, while he ran ashore on the bubbles[8]. Flooding that spring made some of the water so fast it sliced the logs on the way through. All they needed was a mill downstream to collect, sort, and stack the lumber.

This was the year of the famed Round River Drive. The crews had worked all winter notching, sawing, felling, and swamping the trees, then bringing them down the skidways with canthooks, peaveys, and go-devils to the horse-jammer, steam-jammer, or slide-ass jammer, next to the deckers and barkmarkers at the landing, and into the river where the River Rats or River Pigs worked them into booms held with boomsticks for a spring drive. The day finally arrived for the boom to start moving under a favorable north wind; and Paul himself headed the drive.

On the third day they were all astonished to find themselves passing a logging camp, since they had no idea that another was so close. Three days later they passed yet another; and this time they were particularly surprised to discover a large *blue ox* in one of the nearby fields, since nobody had ever dreamed that there was another Babe in all the world.

Then on the ninth day when they passed a camp for the third time, and again saw a *blue ox*, it finally dawned on them that this was their own camp which they had now passed three times! It had simply never occurred to anybody, when dumping in the logs, that this particular river never went any place.

This was also the winter of the False Blue Snow. We will recall that the stuff came down in a natural state – though for unknown reasons – when Paul discovered Babe the Blue Ox. This time it started coming down white, but changed to blue during the following rather remarkable scenario: It seems there was a huge white pine which the notch-cutters had figured right for direction, but not for length. When they dropped it, the fall ran the top all the way back to Camp where it hit the Straw Boss right in the face. This man was not named Foulmouth Falmouth for nothing. When he swore, even scholars gathered from faraway places because of the new languages that came into existence. Now he began swearing a blue streak, such that the very leaves on the trees shook, needles on the pines curled and withered, and the whole pinery began leaning southwest. He was the Paul Bunyan counterpart in the Four-Letter-Word Circuit. He could even spell Massachusetts Institute of Technology with four letters and make the very Angels of Heaven shudder. In fact, as far away as Australia a certain type of large and well-known bird, which always used to strut with its head held high in the air, to a man (bird?) stuck them in the desert sands for protection, developing a habit from which they never recovered.

As Foulmouth kept pouring it out, even the snow turned blue, becoming the same color as the sky, such that the men in charge of skyhooks couldn't tell where to put them. One crew of Road Monkeys cleared a road around a big blue hill in order to keep the grade flat, only to discover the hill disappearing when the wind came up and blew the clouds away.

Foulmouth Falmouth delivers an oratorium on falling trees – with effects registering as far away as Australia.

Fortunately it was so cold that winter that the Pacific Ocean froze over, and they were able to import white snow from China and get on with normal business.

When this spring drive finished, and Paul found himself back at the same camp from which he started, the first thing he did was to get a shave and haircut so he could sit down and think without scratching his lice. His friends did this for him by getting a haymower pulled by a double team of mixed ox/horse – nobody ever explained why. They used a road scraper for giving him a shave, first lathering up a lake by using the water wagon to dump in a load of soap. Then they got ninety-nine of Paul's specially trained cottontail rabbits to run through a big barrel of talcum powder and out across his face while he was lying comfortably on the floor.

About planting time that spring, a strange thing happened. A bunch of ants got into Sourdough Sam's sourdough and "riz" along with it to enormous size. Those ants got so big the 'Jacks had to call them uncles rather than ants. Each one would easily run two hundred pounds with six of its legs still in the air. It was Paul's brilliant idea to give a select set of them a shot of Copenhagen snuff. For an ant-sneeze is strange enough, but an "uncle sneeze" is really something to be reckoned with. Paul built a 20-uncle harness and sent them with a box of snuff out in the field to "sneeze out" the furrows.

About that time a stray dog came into camp; and the reason for his pet name *Koo Koo* will soon become evident. He was part wolf and part hodag, and apparently had been raised on truffles dug up by wild boars. The dog usually slept in the barn. One night Paul thought he heard a 'coon in the warehouse; and he threw his axe with such unerring accuracy that it cut the critter right in two. When he brought in a lamp, he discovered to his indescribable horror that he had cut the Camp pet in two! Paul came by his clumsiness naturally, being so big; and when in his nervously upset condition he put the two

Paul's little demi-canine pet Koo-Koo.

halves of the dog back together and bandaged him with rope, he got the rear end upside down. This was not discovered until the following morning when the 'Jacks came out to survey the scene in broad daylight. It was too late to pull him apart and do it right. And the name of the dog has been *Koo Koo* ever since.

Koo Koo became a marvelous hunting dog because he was perfectly tireless. For he could run on one pair of legs, then simply switch to the other when he got tired. The only serious problem with Koo Koo was that Paul had to hang his pet fire hydrant from the ceiling, with a pan on the floor below.

Another Camp pet that showed up that summer was *Yoo Hoo* the Camp Cow. This was a huge oxen-ess – a female ox – that strolled into Camp one day after hearing Babe bellow. The men immediately made her feel at home because she afforded them a fresh milk supply. She got the name Yoo Hoo from Bowlegs Bronsen calling her "You what" one day, which the other 'Jacks objected to because they thought she was a "who" rather than a "what". One day Yoo Hoo got out in a balsam swamp and ate some of the trees along with the grass. It ruined the milk for drinking, but it made great cough syrup.

They could never get Yoo Hoo to mate with Babe; and she finally left Camp. The 'Jacks had different opinions about this, some of which were very in-teresting. There was general agreement, however, that Yoo Hoo was discouraged by Babe's inordinate love for Camp beans.

After Yoo Hoo was gone, Paul tried to console Babe by making a special harness for him out of *snallygaster* skin, which was remarkable for stretching so greatly when wet. This made it much easier for Babe to do his work. Paul would simply wait for a rainy day, then go out and hook a whole section of pines to Babe's harness. He could now lead Babe back to the landing without his pulling anything, since the harness merely stretched. Next he would take the harness off Babe and put it on a couple of huge steel boom anchors. When the sun came out and the harness shrank, it pulled in the whole sec-tion. The principal problem was that he could only haul on days of favorable weather; and by the time Section 36 got hauled to the river, it often happened that trees had already grown up again on Section 1, so there was no place to put Section 36 when he brought it back. This made what appeared to be a thirty-seventh section in some of the townships; and it was this that caused later loggers to encroach unknowingly on other people's property. They always meant well. They just didn't pay enough at-tention to their own history.

REFERENCES

1. *Bigfoot Baffles Scientific Gumshoes*, Baltimore Evening Sun, Baltimore, MD., p.A3 (14 Jan. 1974); also see Green, J.: *Year of the Sasquatch*, Cheam Pub. Ltd., Agassiz, B.C. 2nd ed., 80 pp. (1970); *On the Track of the Sasquatch*, ibid., 4th ed., 78 pp. (1971)
2. Wade, E. L.: *The Monkey from Alaska*, Harvard Magazine *81*, 48-51 (Nov.-Dec. 1978)
3. Clark, E. E.: *Indian Legends of Canada*, McClelland & Stewart Ltd., Toronto, Canada, xiii + 177 (1960)
4. Danziger, J.: *The Champlain Monster*, Lanser Press, Palinfield, VT., iv + 92 (1981)
5. *Tsawhawbitts the Evil Spirit*, Tourist Information Center, Jarbidge, Nev., 1 p. folder, (ca. 1970)
6. Moon, M.: *Ogopogo: Canada's Loch Ness Monster*, Fate *31*, 34-42 (Nov. 1978)
7. *Scientist Seeks for Dinosaur in Congo*, Pilot-Independent, Walker, Mn., p.13 (3 Dec. 1981)
8. *Brainerd, Minnesota – The Capital of Paul Bunyan Playground Presents First Annual Brainerd Paul Bunyan Exposition*, Souvenir Program, 18 pp (18-20 July 1935)

Look out Babe! Here's that dam fly again!

Lynchia holoptera or "caprimulgid fly" at 25x.
Courtesy Milwaukee Public Museum

CHAPTER VI

PAUL AND BABE GO WEST

For some years Paul continued in the various New England and Canadian camps, finding various ways to make both himself and Babe useful. Once he even served as Walking Boss; and because the Big Man, who was already a legend, particularly favored Swedes for his Foremen because they were trustworthy, loyal, helpful, friendly, courteous, kind, obedient, cheerful, thrifty, brave, clean, and reverent, and had all been trained in the Old Country to help little old ladies across the street, everybody in the camps was soon a Swede:

Nels Nelson
Sven Svenson
Olaf Olafson
Francois Francoison
Kelly Kellyson
Ike Isaacson
Ivanovich Ivanovichson
Umberto Umbertoson
Murph Murphyson
Helmut Helmutson
Pulaski Pulaskison
Ishvar Ishvarson
Helsinki Helsinkison
Heinz Heinzson
Pierre Pierreson
Bologna Bolognason
БВДЕЖЗ son
サイエンス son
אבגדהוזחטיכרלמ son
?!ß£$() son
אבראכרהנא son
البريطاني son
אבגדהוזה son
ثَثَثَجَخَ son
𓂃𓏏𓆑𓅱𓏤 son
科学 son
 son
$\sum\limits_{n=1}^{x} a_n$ son

Meantime Babe had become a real mainstay in the work areas, since he could pull a load of logs otherwise requiring a half-dozen teams. In fact, they often piled the horses on top of the logs to keep them from feeling disgruntled over being left out.

Also, there was a neat problem with rivers where Babe cut his own mustard. All rivers, naturally, flow downward and generally toward the sea. But there are occasions when loggers would like to float their logs in the opposite direction. We have already mentioned how Paul got Babe to drink up the headwaters of the Penobscot to get it to flow back up from Penobscot Bay.

But in the present case Paul fashioned a special kind of waterhook, following the general idea of the skyhook. This he attached to a long rope off Babe's harness with the hook dropped in the river's mouth. On command, naturally, Babe pulled a mighty pull; and up came the mouth so that the river flowed backward. The loggers were doubly pleased. For not only were they now able to send logs both ways on a river, but the fish became so confused on finding themselves swimming upstream downstream, that they took off sideways instead, and right into the buckets and soup pots set by the Cook's flunkeys along the way.

Nevertheless, all good things must come to an end – just as the best of foods and drinks do after entering one's alimentary canal. Besides, two other strong factors were prompting Paul to move, and to move west. First, interesting rumors were continually being brought back by Indians who led fur traders up the Great Lakes and toward the setting Sun, but returned for a spring visit to their beloved sugar bush. Stands of virgin timber, they vowed, were so vast they made the best forests of Maine look like a bowl of toothpicks at a Howard Johnson motel. Three of their own braves, who were being taught to estimate timber by cruisers in camps they supplied with fish and wild rice, missed the trip back east because they were still calculating the board feet from the first tree.

Second, that famous Year of the Quiet Winter, which we earlier mentioned, was soon followed by the worst rainfalls in the history of the State of Maine, where records had been faithfully kept since Noah brought his Ark to Mt. Washington on a good-

Babe reversing the river with a waterhook.

will visit. Rain fell so hard and so long that the water began coming back up from China and washing out trees by the roots. Like the historic Flood Legend itself, many tales of later logging camps come from that time, and much of logging jargon itself. For example, as these great rains increased, they finally got to the point where the water couldn't be contained in drops any more, and began "coming down in buckets".

Now it so happened that at that very time the Church in Quebec unfortunately decided to send a missionary across the international boundary and try saving the pagan Yankees in Paul's logging camp. But the missionary couldn't find the camp because of the rain. Resorting to fervent prayers directed toward Heaven, he finally succeeded in routing out four recently deceased lumberjacks who were not yet too far away. In fact, these former Earth dwellers had been temporarily stationed in a "Triple H" or Heavenly Halfway House, where some more training was still needed to clean up their language. The four lowered an old blanket they had somehow managed to bring with them, got the missionary to climb aboard, then flew him around until he spotted the Camp. The name *Sky Pilot* quickly got attached to this man when the astonished 'Jacks below saw how he arrived from above; and many were his immediate converts.

However, when other missionaries in later years gladly appropriated this same affectionate monicker, it made some of these oldtimers' blood boil. After all,

It rained so hard the H$_2$O came down in buckets.

Four deceased 'Jacks transporting the first sky pilot to Bunyan's logging camp.

it was their own dear deceased buddies who did that piloting. All the other guy did was ride – and pray, of course. In fact, instead of the missionary saving lumberjacks, it was lumberjacks who saved the missionary.

These four old disembodied 'Jacks, by the way, were rather interesting; and at least one of them we have met before. For manning the NW corner of that old blanket, now serving as an E.B. or Ethereal Balloon, was none other than Paul's old friend Foulmouth Falmouth whose language, as we will recall, was so bad that instead of just expletives and adjectives, even his verbs and nouns were 4-letter words. At the NE corner, and holding on for dear afterlike, was River Rat Ralston, whose choice of words was not much better. One Sky Pilot once made the horrible mistake of asking Ralston to read the 23rd Psalm during Ladies Day at Camp 9. He hadn't cleared the first two lines before every last one of the fair visitors had fled camp. Even a recipe that Rat once tried to read out of the Settlement Cookbook, for the il-

literate Sourdough Sam, came out so bad the dough went direct to the outhouse without being eaten.

Seated at the SE corner was Swamper Oldfield Brendenhall, whose initials tell most of his story; and then at the SW was the chief navigator, the Blanket Bull, none other than Minnesota's later famed Pig's Eye Parrant, believe it or not. For Pig's Eye was such a hopeless case that the Governing Board of the Tripe H, sometime after the present episode, sent him back to Earth to try it again. And as any good Minnesotan now knows, when Pig's Eye did come back in the early 19th Century, he set up a saloon near Ft. Snelling which so thoroughly demoralized the entire United States Army that he was kicked off the Reservation. Landing on the opposite bank of the Mississippi about ten miles downstream, Pig's Eye evened the score by founding the Capital City of that State. It would normally have been named St. Peter instead of St. Paul, but Parrant got a bit teed off by his interim experience outside the Gates of Heaven, which we are now about to relate.

Minnesota's Pig's Eye Parrant, who
would subsequently found St. Paul,
gets booted out of Heaven "to try it
again" back on Earth. (It still didn't
work.)

In the first place, this old 'Jack's language was so
bad that even the Chief of the Apostles couldn't
hack it. Largely as an act of desperation, he handed
Pig's Eye a board and asked him to use Braille in
order to save his ears. But the board just sat there
with its wood smoking and the plastic curling.
Worse, it not only routed Old Man Braille himself
out of one of the heavenly storage vaults, but St. Pete
had one helluva time getting him to go back. He was
really burned up.

Now, you cannot swear in Heaven. It's not that it's
against any Holy Writ or Rule; the words simply
don't register. So when St. Peter asked these four
'Jacks the simple, straight-forward, and purely
technical question of what in Hell had they been doing, there was such a prolonged period of silence he
thought they were snobbing his request.

After another sustained period of seemingly useless
and quite exasperating monologue on the side of the
Gatekeeper, he finally told them all to go to Hell.
NOW – *this* they understood; so they went. But what
they could never quite understand was why St. Peter
could use such language and have it register, while
their stuff all got muffled out.

Another interesting thing about these men was
that, after St. Peter told them to go to Hell, they
found themselves instead back at the Heavenly Halfway House, the Triple H. Experiences there had really not been quite that bad. In fact, not bad at all.
Whatever you thought about, there it was – Sourdough Sam's doughnuts stacked ceiling high, bottles
of Scotch running about three firkins apiece, water-
beds in the bunkhouse . . . It was great. Over the next

Rare photograph of George Washington in Paradise crossing the Delaware in a Trident submarine at the
head of a fleet of battleships –

hill a bunch of dead Indians were also apparently having the time of their afterlives chasing uncountable herds of buffalo, while their squaws picked bushels of bright beads off convenient and fast-growing bead bushes. Ralston said he saw a Chinaman in a rickshaw pulled by the Emperor. Even George Washington came through the Triple H, though the visit was brief. And the four 'Jacks marveled as they watched him crossing the Delaware at the head of a fleet of a half-hundred Class-A battleships, Hessian Redcoats on the opposite shore shrieking for their mothers as they raced half-naked and in all directions for the woods, with George himself seated contentedly in a rocking chair, atop the conning tower of a Trident nuclear submarine.

Trouble was that, when you reached out to grab the bottle of Scotch, it faded out. After trying it a few times, these dear guys began to give some serious thought to what the Sky Pilots back at camp had been telling them about Purgatory. Then there came that big event of the mass burial of a whole busload of New York chorus girls who had gone over a California cliff during a road tour. When these four 'Jacks lifted their bag-encircled eyes and looked upon that unforgettable scene of such a rare dish – dish? Smoky the Bear, a platter! – heading directly toward them in the Triple H, they as of one rolled back and nearly laughed themselves sick thinking how they had so thoroughly outwitted the vaunted St. Peter. Great golden balls of fire! They *were* in Heaven, or certainly some very suitable substitute! And to hell with harps, hymns, and the little feathered angels!

– while Hessian Redcoats race in all directions through the woods without taking time to dress, all wildly screaming for their mothers.

In Purgatory you *see* what you want, but you don't get it!

GOODBYE MAINE! The start of the historic move to
Michigan, Wisconsin, Minnesota, and eventually the far west.

BUTT – when each of them reached out to grab a
few as they came within reach, only to have them fog
out and fade away into thin air just like the Scotch, it
began in turn to dawn on all four of them, and as one
man, that all was not roses at the Triple H. They
reached out for a few more legs – *no* soap! In fact, no
legs. It was the Millennium, sunset at the Heavenly
Halfway House. St. Pete was right after all: They *were*
in Hell! For only Satan himself could ever think up
such a totally diabolical misconstruction as a *disembodied woman!*

However, let us now return to the land of the living, and to Paul's camp in that memorable spring
following the frigid Quiet Winter. For still other logging jargon derives from that wet and miserable
season. Forced to stay indoors, the men naturally
became fretful and *peevish.* When some of them finally started a free-for-all fight and grabbed the old poles
they called "log grabbers" to use as weapons, the
results were so disastrous they finally had to sign an
armistice; and the "log grabber" thereafter became
known as a peevie or *peavey.*

One of the braver crews tried to continue logging
despite the torrential downpour. But when the rainwater began to produce its own great rivers, they
only managed to save themselves by dumping their
loaded team and riding the logs into Camp. Those
who made it looked like drowned rats; and when the
floods finally subsided, and the Walking Boss decided
to replace some of the team transportation by river
flotation, he used these marvelously experienced
River Rats to keep the booms in order by riding and

herding strays. And so it is to this day. River Rat
Ralston was one of the 'Jacks in that crew that didn't
make it. But he was honored with the title post-
humously.

By the time the rains subsided, Babe the Blue Ox
was so famished he got out of his pasture and ate
three of their best pineries. This made him definitely
a *persona non grata* – or rather *occubis non grata* –
despite his good traits; and as for Paul, he got on that
same select list because of the smell of his socks. Like
everything else about Paul, his socks were tremendous, and so was their smell – as we had occasion to
mention earlier. It was necessary for him to wash
them in yellow-naptha Camp soap, then dry them
every day; but with it raining all the time, nothing
got dried even if it got washed. Within a couple weeks
the usually tiny fungus called mildew attained the
size of those famous mushrooms later given the taxonomic classification *Kapukis horrendis.* Fortunately
the kapuke gas that arose from them finally killed off
the species; and it is from this original situation that
we now have the word *extinct* from the earlier *ex-
stinked.* All because of Paul's socks.

Thus it was that on the first Green Tuesday after
the third Blue Moon in 54321 B.C. (yes, Virginia, it
was in Paul's Camp that they started the first half of
the Metric System), Paul passed a couple of canthooks through Babe's nose; and these two miserable
outcasts were soon on their way to new pastures, and
a new homeland which – unbeknownst to them, of
course, at the time – would eventually become the
world-famed center for all priceless lore and legend

58

Paul and the redoubtable Babe form the Great Lakes.

on the greatest team and family ever to grace (?) the camps of those loggers whose timber built America. Bunyan and his *Bunyarns* may have originated in Maine, and even blossomed somewhat in Michigan and Wisconsin on the way west; but it was in Minnesota's Lake Region that it all came to its beautiful modern climax. This, of course, was principally due to Paul's marrying an Ojibwe and producing *Gazonk* with his two remarkable brothers, as we shall soon relate.

For Paul himself did little of anything in Minnesota camps that he hadn't already done in Maine. In his case, living that was normal for Paul made legend for everybody else. And this is why stories on the famed folk hero, whether heard around the campfires of Michigan, Wisconsin, Minnesota, Montana and Idaho, or even the Pacific Coast States and Provinces from California to Alaska, are essentially the same. We have simply narrated them here as they happened for the first time, beginning at the beginning, which was on the opposite side of the continent, along the Lower St. Lawrence Waterway from the Province of Quebec to the State of Maine. Thus the legends came to cover essentially the entire Continent of North America, from Atlantic to Pacific. But there it stopped. For although other lands and other peoples have equally fabulous tales spun about fanciful heroes, there is only one Paul Bunyan; and he belongs to the United States and Canada like wild rice belongs to the Upper Great Lakes, shoo-fly pie to Pennsylvania – and Gazonk to Minnesota. For

nobody else ever even heard of Gazonk.

In those days when Paul started heading toward the great Minnesota Northwest, there were no Great Lakes, neither any St. Lawrence Waterway – though there would soon be. For as "Big Foot" Bunyan strode along, followed as usual by the ever-faithful but always-urinating Babe the Blue Ox, his feet sank huge pits into the postglacial sands, and occasionally even into the bedrock. These natural depressions were then promptly filled by Babe to form what we now call the Great Lakes. The water, fortunately, has since cleared up in most of them due to rain and melt run-off from glacial ice, also artesian springs cracked open by Babe's hooves; but one can still occasionally taste something of Babe in Lake Erie.

Of considerable geological interest is that Paul paused momentarily after punching out the lakebeds of Huron and Erie, then turned toward the south to get his face out of the wintry blast of a blizzard blowing at that time, and particularly to knock the icicles off his beard. For as he pivoted a half-turn to point his right foot south, he produced the basin of the later Lake Michigan. Even the pattern of his instep can still be traced on the eastern shore.

We will not put on record how Green Bay got both its form and its name, because of a fine sense of propriety on the part of one of our proof-readers. But every bit of it is true. And it is certainly both historically and geologically accurate to say that the name *Winnebago* for the lake, which in our own time flows into Green Bay but was at one time a part of the Bay itself, is the Algonquian Indian term for a totally undrinkable liquid, essentially meaning "ISH!" The similarly named Winnebago Indians, as another example of this same thing, must have been a notably smelly tribe; and this whole wretched story then reached its climax in a totally unprintable legend as to what happened in our own Lake *Winnibigoshish* in Minnesota, which even made the Indians themselves add another "-ish" to a word which already meant "ISH!".

Now, there is a part of the Bunyan Legend that is indeed novel to that whole area which was broadly called Northwest Territory in the days of the founding of our Country; and this arose from certain friends of Paul's who sooner or later followed him faithfully from the camps of Maine into those of Minnesota, and even beyond. Today every great athletic team in those States belonging to the former Northwest Territory is spoken of in terms of the *Big Ten*. Why Big Ten? Well, hang around and listen:

When Paul left New England he naturally left many dear friends behind; and there were nine of them in particular who were so devoted that they eventually followed him all the way to Minnesota. These rare characters along with Paul then made what historically became called the Big Ten. Not all were physically a match for Paul, of course; nevertheless their deeds were nothing to sniff at. In fact, many of their exploits became so closely woven into the very warp and woof of the great Bunyan tapestry of American folklore – indeed into American history – that it is often difficult today to tell where the one begins and the other ends.

For example, there was *Dutch Olson*, the cookhouse flunky hired to punch out the holes in Sourdough Sam's donuts. Olson got the name "Dutch" because of a disgustingly stingy trick of offering to pick up the bar tab one Saturday night out, in a neighboring town, then wangling it into a Dutch Treat. The *reason* he did this was perhaps to satisfy some deep inner desire to lead a marching band, or – Heaven Forbid! – possibly to win a popularity contest. The *way* he did it, however, was much more interesting. It all began when the last log dropped that late Saturday afternoon, and Olson hollered:

"DRINKS ON ME!"

So practically the whole camp marched behind their hero on the way to town after supper. There Olson grandiloquently ordered a round, then suggested a game of Musical Chairs to increase the merriment. The principal difference between his game and the conventional one was that the same number of chairs kept being used each time – just one short of the number of 'Jacks; and the guy left standing got to call the shot on the next drink.

Finally, and about on the fifth or sixth round, Olson arranged to outfumble the others and be left to name his own poison:

"Double Blue Ox!"

Now, a single Blue Ox – named for Babe, of course – was enough to pull anybody's road straight, corrode even the gold out of your teeth, and put a spinal column right in the want-ad column. So quite understandably the **Double Blue Ox** was simply a saloon version of *Taps* without music. Many a mug was still half full when the mug of the drinker was flat on the floor. As the bodies dropped, and the barkeep was busy mopping up his linoleum, Olson quietly slipped him a few bills covering his own drinks, then disappeared into the night.

Nor was the barkeep any newcomer to this kind of stuff. He was neither born yesterday nor had anything wet behind his ears, except perhaps for a few squusbed woodticks. He simply peeled off the 'Jacks pants so they couldn't walk out of there, hung them on the wall behind the bar with a chit tacked to each, then awaited their awakening. Where a slow response was keeping him up too late, he'd unload a bucket or two of ice into the 'Jack's shirt.

And so it was "Dutch Treat" Olson ever after, or just Dutch for short.

Dutch was still punching when Paul left; and he kept on punching even after Sourdough fell into his own cake mix one day and the dough supply stopped. Between the job and the smell of Sam's typically fermented dough, Dutch became the first person in medical history who was really punch-drunk. He simply didn't notice that neither Sam nor his dough was there any more, and he just kept on punching. Neither did the 'Jacks seem to notice any particular difference after Sam's funeral, when Dutch's continued punching was producing their donuts out of the table top. But they did finally holler like hell when pieces of floorboard started coming through, and the nails got stuck in their teeth.

So they rode Dutch out of camp on a pole – with him still madly punching. They dumped him in the

Punch-drunk Dutch Olson just kept on making donuts even when the dough ran out – and few 'Jacks ever knew the difference.

"Pud" Rollins and his lop-eared lutefisk donuts riding to the
mess table on a squirrel-driven sausage conveyor belt.

Hudson and went back to Maine – little realizing
that they had just invented *donut dunking*. Dutch
made it to shore, picked up the easy scent of Babe,
and continued west, usually paying his way by stopping at Michigan or Wisconsin camps to help in the
cookhouses. Because he had lost his tools in the Hudson, Dutch changed his technique from sledge and
cold chisel to swinging an Indian pogamoggan or war
club at the donut dough spread on the cookhouse
table. Dutch's divot became the donut hole; and thus
was the great game of *golf* born. Indeed these nine
pals of Paul were famous people.

Pud Rollins meantime had developed a fatal fascina-
tion for the Cob Program back at the home camp.
"Pud" got his moniker from the huge animated
sausage he developed. Serving one spring as cookee
on a wanigan with only one flunky named Sloppy
Suppe, who was stone deaf, and not wishing to
engage in unnecessary travel within such tight
quarters, Pud made a special sausage to go with his
justly famous oversize *lop-eared lutefisk doughnuts*. The
sausage was made of the usual smoked heads and
necks of cow, pig, horse, ox, Indian, and occasionally
the amputated legs or arms contributed by the camp
hospital. But instead of using the customary pig gut
for casing, he used ox gut to get bigger sausages. Then
he would stick in an acorn a little over halfway, ram
in a live squirrel so the nut was about an inch ahead
of its nose, slit four holes in the ox gut to let the
squirrel's legs hang out, then pass the weird construc-

tion along to Sloppy with a messy old card simply
reading P.U.D. for "put under doughnut". This the
flunky would do. The squirrel would start sniffing,
shortly scrambling like hell to get the acorn; and one
big lop-eared lutefisk doughnut would be on its way
to the mess table aboard a very choice hunk of
sausage.

As for the squirrels, the 'Jacks merely spit them out
along with the acorn, in the direction of the kitchen,
so Pud could sweep them up and reuse them for that
unlikely situation in which some 'Jack survived the
first helping and still wanted a second. Now about
the cobs:

Old Pog finally taught Pud how to see a cob –
though just one cob at a time. When after long
disciplinary training Pud finally got what he thought
was a matched pair, he brought them one at a time to
a particularly dirty corner in the bunkhouse where
they could shack up and produce little cobs. But as
soon as he got the two together, they became invisible. His cob vision was 20/20, but not 40/40.

So he tried bringing three together, with the idea
that what goes in must come back out: Visible 1 →
invisible 2 → visible 3. This actually worked, except
that he created a classical love triangle by doing it,
and the baby cobs came out triangular. They
couldn't spin a web because what went out came
back in. A triangle is a round trip with straight lines.
Besides, this giving birth to triangular cobs caused
Ma Cob such pain that the yelling and screaming

61

Ol' Pogamoggan helps Pud round up a beautifully matched pair of cobs.

kept the 'Jacks awake all night. Worse, when a cob dies, you can't bury the dead body because you can't see it. You simply have to wait until the smell arrives; and the possibility of breeding sweet-smelling dead invisible cobs seemed unattractively lean. Shortly Pud found himself on the Old Dutch Trail – namely riding a pole out of camp toward the Hudson. He did manage to grab one of his pets on the way, but it drowned during the dunk.

Because no lumberjack ever did see a cob, Pud left them little to remember him by, except perhaps for his invention of the *One-Way Fly*. This story has zip even if no zippers – it was not that kind of fly – and warrants telling. It seems that Pud's eyesight had become remarkably sharp through Old Pog's training; and one day during the brief lunch break in a bug-infested woods, Pud noticed that horse flies, deer flies, black flies, and mosquitoes alike all (1) fly toward a person, (2) pause in a sort of hover as they select their landing site, then (3) either back away by beating the left wing, or bomb straight ahead by beating the right. A nimble man by nature, Pud immediately (a) threw away his fly-swatter, (b) pulled a small scissors out of his bachelor's bag, and – whenever some dam miserable insect flew in to take a bite – (c) lashed out with his scissors and snipped off the right wing. Result: The critter could only fly backwards.

Furthermore, the snipping apparently lobs off the spiral end of some gene hanging out of the gut and into the wing structure, such that the peculiarity becomes an inherited trait. By the end of the logging season the whole woods was still full of bugs, but only the one-way kind, and in the "away" direction. It was an absolutely masterful discovery.

Through some perfectly repulsive coincidence which we will not relate here, the Straw Boss brought Albert Einstein into camp one day; and he spent the whole precious 18 minutes of the lunch break trying to explain that everything is relative: That is, it doesn't make any difference whether the bug goes away from you, or you away from the bug – you don't get bit.

To hell with that stuff! Pud had it fixed so the bugs did all the "away" stuff, leaving the 'jacks to go about their business. And believe me when I say that some of them later sent a very strongly worded letter to the King of Sweden when they heard Einstein got a Nobel Prize instead of Pud.

In Michigan, Pud had the great and good fortune of finding a Michigan cob in one of the camps on the Saginaw. But the crews were cleaner in Michigan than in Maine, and they didn't want cobwebs. So for a while Pud tried his talents at fiddling instead, and became sufficiently good at it to go down in Michigan logging history as *Fiddlefoot Jones*[1]. He also became the founder and principal organizer of the interesting groups known as the Bloodstoppers and the Bearwalkers of Michigan's Upper Peninsula[2].

But this stuff proved quite a drag, compared to Pud's first love with cobs. So he was soon on his way west again, with the last singleton specimen dangling from a cobweb hung around his neck. He made the Grand Portage straight across Lake Michigan to the Door Peninsula, and without his little pet getting drowned from the spray; but as soon as he stepped ashore in Wisconsin, the poor critter's eyes became glassy, and shortly he disappeared so that even Pud couldn't see him. Whether the little fellow died from natural causes, or the increasingly hostile attitude toward cobs that he encountered upon going west, will probably never be known. But to this day it remains a fact that such a thing as a cobweb in the bunkhouses of camps in either Wisconsin or Minnesota remains completely unknown.

Grief-stricken, Pud covered himself with charcoal for mourning, canoed up the Fox and down the Wisconsin to the Mississippi, and then up to the St. Croix. Here he enjoyed a delirious reunion with his old friends Paul and Babe, at that first camp in Wisconsin Territory following the Treaty with the Indians in 1837. But that gets us ahead of our story.

Big Slob Kittell was another of those famous buddies of Paul; and he was the only one who nearly equalled him in size. Slob's father was a famous French-Canadian whose true name is not on record; but his nickname was *Qui-est-elle*, from whence the name Kittell arose phonetically when he came among English-speaking people. This monicker he earned through being an inveterate woman-chaser – always excitedly asking: "Qui est elle?" or "who is she?" whenever anything in a skirt swantzed by. In fact, to this day he holds the Canadian record of having had 127 wives, and the world's medical record for having one child born simultaneously from three of them. This was Paul's friend Slob, more properly called Big Slob on account of his size – which one might expect from his having had three mothers. The end for Slob's lecherous old man came rather suddenly when, with his failing eyesight, he saw Scotland's Black Watch parade by a hundred strong one day, blowing their bagpipes – and dressed in kilts.

When Paul left camp for the west, Slob lingered on for awhile, then built a raft large enough to hold himself and his supplies. He poled it down the Penobscot and into the Atlantic, cut back behind what was then Long Peninsula off the mouth of the Hudson, converting it to the Long Island that we know today. Keeping near shore as much as possible, he scraped and dragged out the Intracoastal Waterway all the way to Florida; visited Disney's Epcot to see what the future would bring; cut across the Gulf and into the Panama Canal which, as we will recall, was formed on the occasion of Paul's baptism; and then poled the Pacific shore up to the Gulf of Tehuantepec. Here he cut a new canal, which has since filled in and disappeared, across to the Gulf of Campeche, from whence he poled once again across the Gulf and up to the mouth of the Mississippi.

Upon landing, Slob thought he would go to work for awhile and get back his land legs; so he got a job in some of the southern logging camps working the slash and loblolly pines. Since other 'Jacks stood only about kneehigh to Slob, he got the name *Toe-Knee*; and because he worked like a beaver, there grew up those wonderful legends around a Tony Beaver[3] in southern logging camps.

Going upstream on Ol' Miss' with a raft was not

Big Slob Kittell and the skinny-wabo alligators in the days of creating Lake Pepin.

easy; and by the time Big Slob got to the mouth of the Ohio, he was so tired he became careless and went up the wrong river. Upon discovering his mistake, he swung his pole around in such exasperation that it not only splashed out a lot of water to form some of Ohio's lakes, but he scraped the surrounding countryside in such a manner that to this day the whole State marks its so-called Serpent Mound as an historic spot. There are also numerous other mounds in Ohio Valley country where he swung his pole, or perhaps stopped to do his you-know-what; and it is fascinating to see modern archaeologists puzzling over these topographic forms, always ascribing them to bands, tribes, or races of primitive men, when actually they were made by just one Big Slob.

Back on Ol' Miss' and again heading north, Slob paused near modern Alton, Illinois, to paint his own peculiar barkmark on the cliffs, just in case his friends might come looking for him. When the explorers Joliet and Marquette came by there in 1673, they were so struck by the horrendous pictographs ninety feet up in the air on an unscalable cliff that Marquette left an historic description which we shall quote in a later volume. The simple barkmark of that great Maine logger became known as the Piasa Monsters; and no Indian ever passed the place without pausing to have a discussion with his spirit guides, and tossing a few wads of tobacco at the foot

Embryo Gelb *alias* Johnny Appleseed heads west "straight as the crow flies" to join Paul and his pals.

of the cliff. Nobody was ever able to figure out how the painter or painters ever got up to do their job at that height on a cliff; but for Big Slob it was just a matter of standing up on his raft, and splashing away with a few panther tails dipped in the blood of a buffalo cow.

Slob finally made it all the way to Minnesota and Paul's camp, which was now up the Mississippi at the mouth of the Rum River. Somewhat like his big pal Paul, Slob naturally left a number of further marks of topographic disarray along the way, which we will not take time to mention except for two. Near the mouth of the Wisconsin, he ran into a bunch of Indians having a real ball chasing what they called "skinny-wabo alligators". The name turned out to be a corruption of the Ojibwe *Ishkoday Wabo* or "fire water", their words for the stuff given them by fur traders to soften them up for a good sale. It got its name because it burned all the way down; and with the very first swig, one usually began seeing the skinny-wabo alligators, which were otherwise never around. Big Slob was unable to see what they were chasing; so they sat him under a tree and gave him a shot.

Caligula! The Indians were right! Skinny-wabo alligators were all over the place! So Slob took his rafting pole and joined the fun. Wallowing back and forth, and whacking both right and left, he soon had the whole bed of the Mississippi splattered from cliff to cliff all the way up to Wabasha's village. The com-

plete mess that he made of that formerly neat and meandering stream became the smeared-out blotch of muddy water named Lake Pepin by later French traders. It should be called Skinny-wabo or Big Slob Lake.

Just before reaching the mouth of the Rum, and about where Minneapolis now stands, this thoroughly fatigued and over-sized 'Jack tripped on one of the tabular sedimentary geological formations while wading with his raft, upending the rocky plates. This formed the fluvial obstruction which Father Louis Hennepin saw in 1680 and named St. Anthony Falls. Obviously it should have been named Big Slob Falls.

Embryo Gelb was at the opposite end of the size scale, but commanded great respect for his nimbleness; and he was a very dear friend of all the other nine. Embryo was so small his mother merely thought she had an early miscarriage – until he got up and walked away. In Maine, Embryo was the principal tree topper, because he could even climb out on a twig. When his pals all headed west, by one devious route or another, Embryo decided to cut it straight and go "as the crow flies". So he simply climbed aboard a crow one day and went. This would have initiated the Air Age centuries earlier except that – oh, well . . . That dam Darius Green!

Actually, Embryo did not go direct to Minnesota, but came down in Ohio because the cherries were ripe, and he loved cherries. He then hiked all the way

"Hawk" Hallquist and team: His WCS (Winter Campaign
Substitute for tobacco) drops the game; Vulch the Buzzard
retrieves; the soup pot gets the mix; and the 'Jacks get sick.

to Minnesota with no other sustenance, merely
chewing cherries and spitting out the pits, right and
left, up and down, in and out. Years later many of
them took growth and marked his whole trail. Some
bookseller's hack, who didn't know apples from
oranges, and for whom the word *cherie* was merely a
French term of endearment, decided to make a fast
buck on these trees and published a bunch of stories
about some mythical character called Johnny Appleseed[4][5]. But it was cherries not apples, and Embryo
not Johnny.

Hawk Hallquist was a long gangling muttonhead
with an unfailing ability to get into a mess with people, but a real genius when it came to animals. He
was the first "vet" on logging records, and became
the cause of this particular designation for an animal
doctor after landing in a camp of Minnesota Swedes.
For they soon became of unanimous opinion that
Hawk was "all vet" on everything he tried to do.
They couldn't believe that he even belonged to the
human race, and certainly was not of their own
proud Aryan stock. When they tried to say he was
not only "all wet", but "wetter than any Aryan" they
ever knew, this finally got picked up by some am-
bitious but unlettered Norwegian horse doctor who

started a training school for animal doctors and called the graduates *veterinarians*.

As for the nickname "Hawk", he got it for having
trained a turkey buzzard to act like a falcon and
retrieve dead meat. This odd-ball situation developed
out of his habitual pipe-smoking. Hallquist would
begin in the fall with reasonably good-smelling tobacco; but nobody could stock enough to last through
the winter at the rate he burned it up. Accordingly,
by mid-winter he was left with the problem of
developing a substitute.

While the secret of what he used for this was never
disclosed, every man in camp soon became fully
aware that the shift had indeed occurred. For the
smell was not only extraterrestrial, but within days
the buildup in the bunkhouse would start knocking
small mice off the rafters, next the larger chipmunks
and squirrels, and finally bats out of the roof chinks
where they normally would be protected. All night
long it was "plop! plop! splash! gluph!" as comatose
little bodies dropped on tables and bunks, into
Cookee's soups and stews or sinking in his bread
dough, occasionally into a lumberjacks' boot not to
be discovered until he tried putting it on the next
morning, and unfortunately every now and then

Hawk makes a slight mistake by leaving the Straw Boss's horse in his Tick Dip too long.

right into the open mouth of some snoring logger.

At first Hawk simply walked around with dustpan and broom while he was smoking, sweeping up the corpses and dumping them in the big pot that the cookee used for stew. But this didn't get the ones that fell into the boots and open mouths. So the brilliant guy got a baby vulture out of the nest of a tree that the 'Jacks felled one spring, made a pet of it, and trained it not only to seek out the smoke-inhalation victims of the Animal Kingdom, but to drop them in cookee's pot. Then in the true spirit of the best falconry, Hawk fastened his oversized, camp-fattened vulture on his wrist with a swamp hook, whereupon "Vulch the Camp Hawk" probably became the first carrion bird that made a man's arm tired carrion it around.

When the whole gang was still in Maine, Hawk endeared himself to Paul by inventing a horse dip for their woodtick problem. The 'ticks in Maine in those days were so bad that every horse had them, and so big that there could only be one or two to a horse. Before Hawk came to the rescue, the loggers simply left the 'ticks to dig in, go to work, and puff up. Then the 1-tick horses they sold overseas to Egyptians for one-hump camels, and the 2-tick for two-hump

camels. This stuff about "dromedaries" being a species of their own is taxonomic hernia. De-tick 'em, and you got nothin' but an American horse.

Now, Hawk had heard brief passing mention of something called "sheep dip" used by ranchers in Montana, though nobody seemed to know the formula. This forced his own genius to the light of day; and soon the famous old Camp 9 had a vat full of stuff that smoked and fumed in a most frightful manner, such that it even scared the lumberjacks. Everybody really expected it to blow up. But it sure did the job on the 'ticks: Not only killed them, but *dissolved* them. Everything went fine as frog's hair for quite a long stretch.

Then at the very time that Paul took off toward the setting Sun, the Straw Boss rode into camp with a real crop on his pet horse. He looked like he was padded with baseballs, and the lumps were wearing holes in the rider's pants. Hawk made up a fresh batch and dropped the horse into it. But – Paul's departure distracted him so, that he forgot the usual careful scheduling while waving goodbye. By the time he had wiped the tears off his face, the 'ticks had not only disappeared, but so had the Boss's horse.

If Hawk had stopped with his justly famous horse

66

Beermug Sveeggen had the fortunate experience of coughing out both lungs from Hawk Hallquist's tobacco fumes, so's he had to get his air from beer suds.

dip, and the satisfaction of being one helluva good horse doctor, he'd still be in Maine. But the floorboard nails in Dutch Olson's donuts had understandably caused some real havoc with camp teeth; and a few months after Dutch's inglorious ride to the Hudson, various 'Jacks began coming down with really terrible toothaches. Jowls Jackson finally got so delirious with pain he went to the Camp Vet, not knowing where else to go. Since he begged for *anything* that might help, Hawk naturally thought of his horse dip. So he cautiously inserted a spoonful in Jowls' jowls.

As even a boob should have expected, given any time for thought, the reaction was not only immediate but terrific. However, no matter how much thought one had given it, even a genius would not be likely to predict exactly what kind of reaction it turned out to be. For instead of dissolving the tooth, it dissolved Jowls' *uvula* – perhaps because it looked more like a 'tick than a tooth. This led to the rest of the stuff being immediately shot down the esophagus. Just as immediately, this flicked the switch on the sphincter leading from stomach to duodenum; there next developed violent peristalsis, flagellation, and whiplike sinusoidal action throughout all 32 feet of upper and lower colon, intestine, bowel; then it triggered the anal puckerstring – and OUT! *Timing*: A world record for the 50-yard dash compressed in 10 yards of intestine. *Result*: The horrendous back-draft with its Torricelian vacuum pulled out the bad tooth! Who would have guessed?

While this sounds like a possible success story, it was definitely not so outside of dentistry. For Jowls was never quite the same again. Far worse, nobody could ever find the tooth; and the Tooth Fairy was accordingly unable to leave the usual dime under Jowls' pillow. This made Jowls and everybody else in camp hopping mad; and since the Olson-Rollins pole was still lying around camp begging for use, and the Hudson still flowing, "Hawk the Vet" was soon on his way west to join his pals.

While the camp did lose a good Vet, they picked up at least one compensating benefit. For it used to take at least three chore boys to shovel the stuff out the back door when the 'Jacks sat around on the deacon's seat and it became Hawk's turn to tell a story. After he was gone, it took only one.

Beermug Sveeggen, *Plebe Stout*, and *Chink Wieland* were three of a kind, in that they traveled so widely and started so much of our minor-league folklore. Beermug was a congenial guy, liked by everybody; while Plebe – also called Iron Man – had a pair of hiking legs that simply never gave out; and these two set out together for the southwest not long after Paul left.

Beermug Sveeggen's nickname was originally spelled *Biermug* because he was always coughin'. But after he coughed out both lungs one night when Hawk Hallquist had shifted to his WCS (Winter Campaign

Beermug finds himself in tight quarters – BUT-T-T ➤

Substitute for pipe tobacco), he stopped coughing because he had nothing left to cough with. It was a miraculous cure; and it was this probably more than anything else that influenced the 'Jacks not to run Hawk out of camp earlier. However, Biermug could no longer breathe either, because he had nothing to breathe with; so he took to gulping down beer suds and getting his air that way. This, of course, required an unusually large mug, and an awful lot of beer. Those who came new into camp the following year quite naturally thought "Biermug" was "Beermug". And so it has been ever since.

Furthermore, Sveeggen's face in profile looked remarkably like a 5-liter Bavarian stein, with its large curved handle almost exactly matching his floppy cauliflower ears.

Paul always remembered Beermug for his strange behavior, come nightfall. Drinking so much beer all day, just to breathe, naturally made Sveeggen a little wobbly by sundown. He had been some shakes as a gymnast in his earlier years; and even in later life his favorite exercise to loosen up his muscles before going to bed was to chin himself 40 or 50 times from a rafter in the bunkhouse. Being a big man, his feet would barely clear the floor – perhaps by six inches. But Beermug would have such a load on by that time he'd forget where he was after about the first dozen pull-ups.

"How far is it to the ground?" he'd holler, when about ready to drop. Naturally, no lumberjack was

– he was used to being tight anyway, so's he solved this one in a real hurry.

going to pass up an opportunity like that.

"**Great golden balls of fire**!" they'd yell, more or less in frightening unison.

"Remember you're hanging out a third floor window! Hold everything until we get a ladder!" And of course Beermug would not only remember, but very clearly.

As seconds purposefully passed into minutes, with these in turn soon pushing a full quarter-hour and no ladder yet in sight, even Beermug's muscles naturally began giving out.

"**Hurry dammit!** I gotta let go!"

"No! No! You'll kill yourself!" came back the excited response. "We'll have a ladder here as soon as we can hitch up the team and drive into town!"

At about that point Beermug would start reciting everything he could remember from his childhood Rosary, add a few urgent requests variously directed to the Archangel Gabriel, Zoroaster, or the Lord Buddha, then shut his eyes, grit his teeth – and let go!

About an hour later, it would finally dawn upon Sveeggen that he had not passed over, but was still back on Earth. So he would start unwinding his knees from under his chin and climb into his bunk, an absolute religious convert because of his obviously miraculous rescue, though he could never be quite sure which religion it was.

When Beermug set out with Stout on that sad farewell-to-logging day, he went into cattle-raising on the big Texan ranches; and to make himself popular with the Mexican element, he called himself Pecos Bill. Legends on Pecos Bill[6] are accordingly now legion. His skin, however, responded so quickly to tanning that he soon became embarrassing to the former Confederate Army Officer running the ranch.

Whereupon good-natured Ol' Beermug simply recrossed Ol' Miss' and, figuring that if you can't lick 'em join 'em, he sauntered through Louisiana, Alabama, and the Carolines, sitting with the young people as the venerable negro Uncle Remus[7], and occasionally using his massive strength where needed, under the simple pseudonym John Henry[8].

One fine day Beermug got the characteristic idea – characteristic for him – of going hunting for mountain lions in a mangrove swamp. Strangely enough, however, he found one – rather it found him. For it seems that in those days there was a man-eating beast in the hills renowned for its size and ferocity; and on this occasion it had run out of local residents to eat, so came down to get a few alligators.

However, in that particular swamp was the world's largest alligator – some 27 feet 8-3/4 inches in length when not covered with flies. Beermug was preparing to leap a ditch when he saw this monster on the other side, directly facing him, jaws wide open for the reception. He was about to back out of there, but quick, when he heard an earth-rocking growl immediately behind him. Turning, he found himself confronting the largest lion in Alabama, preparing for a quick meal. The lion leaped; Beermug ducked; the lion kept going right across the ditch – and into the alligator's waiting mouth. Except it was not waiting quite for that kind of a dish.

Given this half-moment of respite – and Beermug

never needed more than half a moment to do all the thinking of which he was capable – he himself leaped the ditch, kicked the lion in the butt to get him really stuck tight in the gator's throat, chopped the hind ends off both of them, then sauntered slowly about his business, leaving it up to other hunters to figure out what in cry-eye had actually happened.

When Beermug leaned over a small pool, however, to refresh himself with a drink after this rather frightening experience, he noticed that he no longer had the color qualifying him to play the part of an Uncle Remus or a John Henry. He had turned pure white. So instead of going back to his new friends, he set out dead northwest to join his old pals in Minnesota.

Along the way he paused in Kentucky for sampling some of their famous applejack; and he decided to stay awhile, probably because he was unable to get up. His exploits shortly built up the famed Old Sol Shell[9] legends of the Kentucky mountaineers.

From there to Minnesota it was by river and by rail. He made the first stretch taking on various odd jobs with steamboats, shortly generating the fantastic Mike Fink legends[10]; and for the second and last leg, he got the job of firing the boiler of the winning locomotive on that most famous of all railroad races. Casey Jones[11] got the epitaph, but Beermug got the ticket.

Plebe meantime had left Beermug to go farther west, working in both oilfields and logging camps. His great boyhood hero having been the financier J.P. Morgan – in days when he was having trouble raising an honest nickel himself – Plebe adopted that name to give him luck. And forever after American folklore has been enriched by tales of a so-called Gib Morgan[12] in the great oilfields of the southwest, and Kemp Morgan[11] in ranching and logging. They were the same guy; and the name wasn't Morgan.

As Plebe slowly worked north to rejoin his old pals of the Big Ten, he somehow or other generated the legends of *Febold Feboldson*[13] in Nebraska. Apparently some big stupid Swede, who thought himself a writer, tried to record the doings of a man which were so fabulous he himself was called "Fable" or Febold by his local admirers; and of course to a Swede even a man named Biche would have to be designated as the son of Biche. So it became Febold Feboldson.

Interestingly enough, it seems that Plebe had the same liking for cherries as did Embryo Gelb, also that he had heard the rumors of a Johnny Appleseed without knowing that it was really his old friend. So one day he was walking the Nebraskan brushland hunting elk, gun over his shoulder and a crate of cherries under his arm, chewing like mad and spitting the stones into a bag to give to Johnny Appleseed in case the dear guy ran out of apples. Suddenly Plebe looked up and found himself confronted by a very stately stag. Quickly and quietly he laid down the crate, and tamped a heavy charge into his trusty gun. But, cursed be the day! he was out of shot!

Without hesitating a moment, however, Plebe tossed a fistful of his cherry pits into the barrel, took his usually deadly aim, pulled the trigger, and landed a load right on the stag's forehead. Unfortunately, cherry pits are not bullets. They scoured his scalp a

Plebe Stout about to bring down a haunch of vension complete with cherry sauce.

bit, and lodged under the skin; but the skull remained intact, and handsome Mr. Stag galloped away.

About two years later Plebe was in this same hunting ground when lo! the same huge stag! But now it was sporting a fully grown cherry tree in the place of antlers; and this tree was loaded with his pet fruit. Plebe was taking no chances this time. He put all his powder and every piece of lead he had in his muzzleloader, including some he was always alleged to have in his butt. Not only did the stag drop immediately upon the first discharge, but his huge juicy haunch came down covered with cherry sauce because of the barrage of extra shot; and it was fully cooked and ready to eat because of the extra charge of powder.

When Plebe began nearing Minnesota, the remarkable winter of '77 was closing in. For several days he fought a blizzard and continually accumulating snow; and although his own legs would have kept on going all the way to the North Pole, his horse was rapidly pooping out. So he tethered him to a rather odd-looking post that was conveniently sticking out of the snow, then laid himself down in a drift to sleep some of it off.

While Plebe was no Rip Van Winkle, he did take a nap that was sufficiently long to last through the blizzard, also the subsequent thaw which removed most of the snow. When he finally shrugged himself awake, pulled himself up on a wet elbow, and blinked a half-dozen times to recover from his snow-blindness, he was astonished to find himself in a churchyard on the outskirts of a small village. So

Plebe Stout unties Bucephalus from the tethering post after the terrible "Blizzard of '77".

70

Chink Wieland of Bunyan's camp on the Penobscot, in days of his youth when he rescued Napoleon from the War of 1812 in Russia.

what sense did that make? Was he dreaming? Had he been kidnapped?

While wheels of that sort were buzzing in his head, Plebe thought he heard his old equestrine pal whinny. But where? Up? He looked up where the whinny came from; and there was none less than old Bucephalus dangling by his tether from the church steeple! No wonder that tethering post had looked a bit odd-ball. When it finally dawned on Plebe that he had slept through some of southern Minnesota's famous changeable weather, he dropped a fat slug in his old muzzle-loader, shot the tether rope in two, then helped his old pal Bucephalus pull his legs out of the ground after landing.

Chink Wieland got his name because he looked like a Chinaman. Actually he was a German named Karl Friederich Hieronymous, Freiherr von Münchausen, who learned how to hop in Australia, chase women up and down the Russian steppes, eat tortillas in Nicaragua, and log in America. Chink was a member of the Royal Chasseurs with Napoleon during his invasion of Russia in 1812. On the flight back, it was his six-horse caisson that the Little Emperor chose for his hectic and historic getaway. Chink rolled off the big gun, tossed a bale of straw on the buckboard for Napoleon, mounted himself between the two big wheels with his feet on the bailiwick and braced against the providion, savagely bull-whipped the butts of his six frothy-mouthed steeds – and headed for Gay Par-ee!

Forty-five miles out of Moscow the snow-covered road entered the Black Forest. An early dusk had long since gone into pure black night. Snow was falling; the Emperor was getting a terrible case of chills on his blains – the first attack of those chilblains which finally felled him on St. Elba; the six great steeds were showing signs of massive fatigue.

All of a sudden the spine-chilling howl of huge wolves in mass chorus! These were the dread *Borscht Wulfen* of the Black Forest, which lived only in the deepest recesses along the boundary between the Russian *Chernaya Dubrava* and the German *Schwarzwald*. They were far larger than any American timberwolf, and much more ferocious. Before you could say "Schiltz," a six-pack dashed out of the black depths, each heading for a separate horse. Their methodical and deadly brilliance was incredible. In mere seconds, each had his fangs sunk into the buttocks of the horse of his choice, and soon great pieces of flesh were being torn away. As the slashing ivory knives moved up into thigh and croup, the tails fell off. No wolf eats a horse's tail. Instead they drove down into the stifles, the gaskins, hocks, cannons, pasterns, fetlocks, coronets. At that point the hooves dropped off; and of course the beasts let these go. Pickled pig's feet, yes; but these weren't pigs, and they weren't pickled.

By this time the horses had no hindquarters, of course, and were running only with their forelegs. But this was compensated by the fact that each horse

Chink Wieland and his faithful pointer Schmutz performing their classic feat on Penobscot Bay.

had the four legs of a wolf driving him along. Their mouths grew white with froth; and this admixed with snow and wolf-banquet splash struck Chink in the face, also loused up the Emperor's parade hat, which he had earlier donned for the great prospective event of marching through the streets of Moscow.

On rushed the frightful and thoroughly frightened team through the Black Forest. With the hindquarters devoured, the voracious jaws moved back up into the croup and haunch, flank and loin, ribs and withers. Fortunately the faithful horses remained in their forward harness, while the rearward parts dropped on the wolves. Still galloping with their forelegs, they now began, however, to enter the serious condition of not having any belly to keep them supplied with energy. And the wolves kept gulping down yet more flesh. These beasts did not even know how to spell "satiation" in Russian. They chewed into the shoulders and breasts, elbows and forearms, knees and cannons, pasterns, fetlocks, coronets – and now the front hooves dropped off. The horses had nothing left to run with – though the wondrously faithful and highly trained beasts still kept frothing at the mouth and pointing toward Paris.

Throughout all this, the great Chink, afterwards knighted Baron von Munchausen – without the umlaut because of the great respect in which he was ever after held – kept tight and unwavering grasp on the reins, driving on his six animals whether horse, or half-horse and half-wolf, or all wolf. The only time he ever looked back was to kick the Emperor in the hat once in a while, to get him to lie down and shut up. There was just the one problem that, although the wolves had dropped fully into the harness upon finishing the forelegs, they still were not wearing the bridle and headstraps. Despite his great prowess in riding stables and out on the hunt, Chink found it difficult to steer a head that didn't have a body, and lash his message into a body that didn't have a head.

But with a great stroke of his usual genius, Chink began lashing the buttocks of the wolves in Morse Code, telling them in Russian that they should finish their good meal with dessert. The wolves responded, drove ahead for those last delicious bites of neck and throatlatch, pole and ear, forelock, nose, mouth, nostrils, face, cheek and jaw – whereupon the teeth dropped out and the horses completely disappeared.

Now Chink once again found himself with a team of uniform, even if a bit unusual, composition – all wolf; he leaned into his whip-lashing with the last ounce of strength at his command; and – *Vive la France!* – daylight could be seen breaking through the heavy branches ahead; the forest was definitely thinning; they were emerging from the dread *Schwarzwald*; they were home again!

Vive le Baron Chink!

In the American logging camps, Chink didn't show up so well merely because he was outclassed in the tight discipline of spinning outright fabrications.

72

Anybody and everybody went into eclipse with Paul around. The one thing that Chink did which achieved at least local fame was to develop a bird dog that would go into "point" at a distance of 300 miles from his target. This meant that the critter was in constant point, even when asleep. The legend at hand arose from the time when Chink brought him along riding a boom down to Penobscot Bay, and "Schmutz" pointed out to sea!

Because everybody went into a high fit of laughter over this obvious boob-off, of what they always believed anyway was a vastly overrated mutt, Chink got sore and began taking bets. None of his friends would match his money because they thought it both embarrassing and unfair, and particularly so when Chink in high dudgeon refused the smart-pants offers from disbelievers running odds as high as 1000 to 1, and insisted on meeting them 1 on 1, or even 1 on 10 himself.

Right in the midst of this loud hassle, with Schmutz still crouched at the end of the dock and his tail looking like a nightstick, there was a big commotion near one of the boats anchored out in the bay. You could hear the firing of a harpoon gun. Shortly thereafter a very excited crew came ashore with an enormous shark, which they then promptly proceeded to slice for barreling the oil. Schmutz seemed inordinately excited about all this, slowly pivoting on his belly to keep his nose beamed on the boat. Suddenly all the businesslike action of shark dissection turned to wild merriment.

For lo! inside the shark's stomach were six braces of partridges, and all still alive! In fact, one was nesting five eggs; and a tiny partridge chick starting pecking his way out of one of them at the very time that the sailors were cleaning them off. It was a great day for Schmutz, Chink, Chink's friends, the partridges – indeed, everybody but the shark, and those embarrassed disbelievers who had bet against Schmutz. The result was that Chink hit it pretty rich; and shortly after Paul had hoisted his pants for the west, so did Chink and Schmutz.

"E.T." Arnold was the last of the Big Ten; and although he was the one who later discovered flying saucers, the "E.T." did not stand for "extraterrestrial". Instead it meant "extra terrible"; and he gained this monicker as follows:

Actually, Arnold came from a fine family with a long line of illustrious forebears. Unlike other 'Jacks, whose socks had no heel reinforcement, and coats had no arms, Arnold was well-heeled and even had a Coat of Arms – three gophers rampant on argyrol. His father was English, though a son of Madame Pompadour – illegitimate, of course; she was in turn the questionable daughter of the great Russian Igor Beavor, outcast son of the Croatian Pssst, who was said to have been sired by Charlemagne during an overnight stop of the Crusades; and of course Charley was the son of Carmelita, daughter of Nero, son of Polycritus, son of Cleopatra, daughter of Ichabod Crane, son of Nebuchadnezzar, son of Genghis Khan, son of Rebecca, daughter of Enoch, who was seventh in line, we will recall, from Adam and Eve.

Arnold's main problem – indeed his only one – was his peculiar penchant for making everybody sore as

Lover-boy "E.T." Arnold clearing out the bunkhouse with his rendition of *The Star Spangled Banner.*

hell. Seated on the deacon's seat around the old Franklin stove one Saturday night, in preparation for celebrating the Camp's day of rest on Sunday, the 'Jacks decided to take turns singing songs. Only a couple had arisen, singing a few delightful but bawdy ditties picked up at the saloon, when it came Arnold's turn. He promptly lit into the *Star Spangled Banner.* The fun was over; a great idea suddenly died; the lights got doused; and the Camp sacked down.

Some months later a couple of the men thought they'd try it again, but definitely avoid any singing. For those were precious moments, seated around the old fire on a Saturday night with their boots off and shirts opened, after a tough 6-day week. They decided to discuss numbers – favorite numbers; and each 'Jack was asked to name his, and tell why it was his favorite. Sloppy Slavinski started off. His favorite was "1" – simply because he had never learned to count. Boondocks Schmidt liked "7" because it seemed kind of mysterious, and probably brought luck. Schnozzle Durante had been hooked on "3" ever since he took some strawberry blond to a ballgame and she struck him out. It was Arnold's turn. His favorite number, naturally, was 3928405968709283746502827365393049586739405921375058398765234819223948573658392013486739382736201938576630918590948372039482039576620394766493049382039886750293848571029380391039576839102573929485721039678 4. The game was over; another great idea suddenly ended; the lights got doused; and the Camp sacked down.

But the thing that really dumped Arnold was the Fiddlin' Bee. The gang was in Camp 10 at the time; it was springtime at its finest; and the foreman, Foghorn Faust, got the really tremendous idea of hauling a wanigan-load of women down from the nearest town for an outdoor Sunday afternoon Fiddlin' Bee. The idea would have been historically great – if it could ever have gotten off the ground. But Arnold with his characteristic prevision and thoroughness prepared himself while everybody else merely waited for the event. The ladies arrived, took their seats on the hastily prepared benches around a sawdust-covered dance area; the fiddling started – and everybody just sat there in a state of frozen silence. After all, these 'Jacks had been confined in Camp all winter, and here they suddenly found themselves looking at a bunch of women. The ladies sensed what was on their minds; the 'Jacks sensed that the ladies sensed right; and if any man among them had actually stepped forth to offer his hand in dance, the action would have been so thoroughly misunderstood that everything wearing a skirt would have been in full flight, literally airborne, toward the wanigan.

But Arnold instead calmly arose and announced to the astonished ladies that he had the local franchise for the famous Valentine dresses. Quickly passing a couple of illustrated catalogs among them, he unrolled his tape and offered to take orders. Powdered noses bent excitedly over the pictures, dainty dishpan hands began going up in the air, the woods started to ring with feminine squeals and wardrobe questions.

Soon Arnold had a fair one standing before him. She had been simply dying over a period of three years to have a dress like the one on page 14. As Arnold began to measure her waist, the eyes of every 'Jack disclosed more and more pupil, then the whites, and finally the backside of the retina. When he began taping the posterior, their jaws dropped, and they drooled all over their shirts. And when he next nonchalantly measured her bust, every 'Jack in the Camp fell flat on his face in the sawdust.

And thus the afternoon passed. Nobody heard much beyond that first squawking of the couple old fiddles that Foghorn had dug up from somewhere. The only one among them who was doing any fiddling was Arnold; and he wasn't using a violin. Perhaps there was some semblance to his playing a bass viol as he passed his arms hither, thither, and yon over female torsos while his erstwhile buddies writhed in agony. They could stand the hither and the thither, but the yon really got them.

When the Walking Boss came through Camp 10 a few weeks later with the employee rating form, which management used as a criterion for rehiring the coming fall, Arnold got his "E.T.". For on the page which rated one's fellow 'Jacks on the basis of personality, popularity, and general ability to get along with others, there were three columns of very elementary sort, designed for the typically uneducated loggers. In the first you simply entered a plus sign "+", which

Arnold puts the finishing touches on earning this monicker "E.T." – Extra Terrible.

meant that the person belonging to that particular name on the list was definitely a good one to have around. A circle "0" in the second column indicated a so-so sort of chap; and if one lifted the crossbar of the "+" to form a "T" in the third column, that letter stood for "terrible".

When the sheets were finally gathered, Arnold was found not only to have a "T" from every 'Jack in Camp, but every one of them with the single excep-tion of Sloppy Slavinski had also prefixed an "E" for "extra". Sloppy, we will recall, never did know there was an "E".

So "E.T." Arnold it was, is, and forever will be. Nor did he get invited back to Camp. How he got out west to rejoin his other odd-ball pals of the Big Ten is nobody's business. But even Indian squaws love Valentine clothes.

REFERENCES

1. Jordan, P. D.: *Fiddlefoot Jones of the North Woods*, Vanguard, 209 pp (1957)
2. Dorson, R. H.: *Bloodstoppers and Bearwalkers*: Folk Traditions of the Upper Peninsula, Harvard Univ. Press, Cambridge, 305 pp (1952)
3. Brown, C. E.: *Paul Bunyan and Tony Beaver Tales*, Pub. by author, Madison, Wisc., 18 pp (1930)
4. Stevens, H. B.: *Johnny Appleseed and Paul Bunyan*, Baker Press, Boston, 92 pp (1931)
5. Atkinson, E.: *Johnny Appleseed*, Harper Bros., New York, 341 pp (1915)
6. Bowman, J. C.: *Pecos Bill*, Whitman, Chicago, 296 pp (1937)
7. Dobie, J. F.: *Paul Bunyan*, National *121*, 237-8 (1925)
8. Johnson, G. B.: *John Henry: Tracking Down a Negro Legend*, Univ. No. Carolina Press, Chapel Hill, N.C., 155 pp (1929)
9. MacKaye, P.: *Tall Tales of the Kentucky Mountains*, Doran, New York, 185 pp (1926)
10. Blair, W. and Meine, J. F. (ed. by): *Half Horse Half Alligator*, Univ. Chicago Press, Chicago, ix + 289 (1956)
11. Shay, F.: *Here's Audacity!*, Macauley, New York, 256 pp (1930)
12. Dorson, R. M.: *American Folklore*, Univ. Chicago Press, Chicago, 328 pp (1959)
13. Meine, F. J.: *Tall Tales of the Southwest: 1830-1860*, Knopf, New York, 456 pp (1930)

Babe, pasturing on the divide near the Minnesota/Dakota boundary, forms some of our principal river systems.

CHAPTER VII

PAUL BECOMES A
FAMILY MAN

Nothing ever struck Paul's fancy better than the incredibly beautiful stands of Minnesota pine; and there he plunked down to stay. Tying a rope around Babe's neck so he could travel no more than a couple hundred miles in each direction, Paul put him out to pasture. The situation was ideal. For Babe only grazed on trees under a hundred feet high, lest one get stuck in his throat. That left the really good stuff for logging.

As the years rolled by, Babe's hoofprints began punching out quite a pattern, which soon filled up with rainwater – and you know what else. In fact, Babe's kidneys were such a totally remarkable construction that he himself, without any outside help whatever, was able to produce one of the world's greatest river systems – the Mississippi. Babe usually relieved himself near his tethering pole at Lake Itasca; but on one occasion he found himself so far away to the southwest, at the end of his rope, that he laid down for the night on what has since become the continental divide near Brown's Valley. By the time the sun rose, there was not only the Minnesota River running off to one side of him, eventually to join the Mississippi, but also the Red River of the North running down the opposite side, and in the opposite direction. He must have rolled over during the night.

As for Paul, his increasingly big problem was loneliness. Brother! was it quiet – nothing but loons calling summertime, and wolves howling wintertime. The logging industry was still far away from Minnesota.

However, there were plenty of Indians running around. Yes, indeedy, there were plenty of Indians. And they had their own means for having fun. It is a strange and tragic thing today to hear people speak so ignorantly of the Indian *Pow Wow*. For this is not the right spelling at all, and it ruins a beautiful piece of history that warrants preserving.

That is, every tribe of Indians since time immemorial has had its periodic community gathering, variously to celebrate religious rites, marriages, and

feats of strength or daring-do in times of war. No tribe in North America ever called such a gathering a "pow wow" until Paul came along.

On the occasion now in question, it was a great celebration of a recent war between the Mdewakanton Sioux and the Ojibwe, on the occasion of driving the Sioux off Mille Lacs Lake. Paul was an invited guest at the Ojibwe camp at the time. Each warrior took his turn, first puffing the calumet, then striking a special stake stuck in the ground according to their custom; whereupon the man would narrate his deeds while the others admiringly, or at least respectfully, listened. Courtesy – always a strong mark of the Indian character – in due time required an invitation to be extended to Paul also, to "strike the stake". Paul obliged; but not having been in the war, he really had nothing of consequence to relate so far as he himself could judge.

So he decided merely to recite a few old tales from his logging days in Maine. The time was now about 11 a.m., the celebration having begun the previous evening at sundown. Even his introduction was impressive. For when he arose, of course, half the place went under his shadow, causing every child in camp to flee into the woods, howling with fright all the way. Upon taking his few pulls on the calumet, the dense clouds of smoke made the squaws so sick they had to excuse themselves; and when Paul finally "struck the stake", and the whole *wigiwamigan* fell down, every Brave in the circle leaped to his feet in undisguised admiration and hollered:

PAUL! WOW!

Paul never got to tell about logging. Drums began pounding; the Indians danced and yahooed in a great circle around their demolished conference hall; and the repeated yelling of "Paul! WOW!" went on throughout the day and the following night. His tremendous effect on the entire Indian culture shows in the subsequent development of their own Bunyanesque legends fashioned after Paul; and those who have not read at least the Ojibwe narrations on *Nana-bozho*[1][2][3][4][5][6][7] should certainly do so. How any dumb klunk historian – or more probably a newspaper editor – ever got "*pow* wow" out of "*Paul! wow!*" we'll never know.

Now, being the all-man he was, Paul found himself needing a mate in those days – and real bad. It didn't help any, either, to hear the meese (mooses?) howling all night during their rutting season. The problem was that he sure needed one moose of a woman.

One fine day while pulling a few logs into his campsite with Babe the Blue Ox, Paul stopped in utter (udder?) astonishment. There at the lakeside and not far from his hut was without doubt the biggest and most remarkably fair-skinned Indian squaw he had ever seen. She was a perfect 36-26-36 – in *yards*! She was for *HIM*! but YES! Paul's admiration mounted by leaps and bounds as the fair maiden began dipping her huge *mokocks* or birch-bark buckets (sorry, pal!), visibly lowering the lake level. When she picked up a ten-foot piece of tamarack driftwood to pick her teeth, he could hardly stand it.

Her name proved to be '*Che-Washi-Wobble*, or what would best translate from Ojibwe into English as Great Belly Dancer. And indeed she was just that.

Paul meets the future Mrs. Bunyan, the demure 11-ton '*Che-Washi-Wobble*, while she is bathing in Sandy Lake.

Priceless photograph of the greatest military strategy in Ojibwe history – defeat of the Sioux at Sandy Lake through distraction by 'Che-Washi-Wobble.

Paul didn't need to know Ojibwe, and 'Che-Washi-Wobble didn't need to know English. They communicated perfectly. All the Braves in her tribe, of course, had the same reaction as Paul's: When 'Che washi, they all wobbled. Hence the name.

On the present occasion she was apparently bathing, and in accepted Indian style was bare to the waist. As Paul watched in rapt admiration, she leaned forward to pick up a piece of soap she had dropped; and a pair of her very generously constructed parts hung down into the water. Immediately every red-blooded male fish in the entire lake leapt a full axe-handle into the air, either clacking his teeth or singing with sheer joy, or both.

Not even a 10-foot electric eel could have produced such an effect on those fish. But then, in the present case, the jump was purely voluntary, not involuntary, with each fish calling upon reserves it didn't even know it had. And to this day the most successful of all fishing lures is the wobbler, fashioned by some smart Indian after that part of 'Che Washi's anatomy which hung in the water, thereby attesting to the accuracy of the legend.

Paul began moving gradually toward the shore even more entranced than the fish, his huge frame behaving like a mere steel buckshot in the presence of a 5-megagauss cobalt-nickel magnet. Interestingly enough, he had his peavey with him – which was particularly fortunate now that he wanted to hold on to something for support. This and his training on

79

cruising timber did finally arouse his torpor long enough to make a couple of quick estimates: First, even trimmed of her limbs she would run a good 1700 board feet – and of exceedingly choice stuff. Second, a sly horizontal sighting with his lifted peavey, while 'Che Washi was busy wobbling, showed she was a full pole-length across the spigots, or approximately two and a half axe handles. It was a stunning sight – yes indeed, stunning.

In fact, at one time the Tribe had even used 'Che Washi Wobble as a secret weapon against the Sioux. The scene was Sandy Lake on the Upper Mississippi in 1761. This was after the Battle of Mille Lacs, and the Sioux had been driven south to the Crow and Minnesota Rivers. But now a strong raiding force had worked its way back to their old homeland, and had silently disposed themselves around Sandy Lake during the night. By dawn the Ojibwe came to know that an enemy was somewhere in the thickets on Brown's Point; but in those days before the North West Company had built their fur-trade post there, the growth was too dense to sight the bodies. Virtual extinction seemed to face the Ojibwe once the Sioux decided to open their attack.

So the famed *Kwiwisensish* or Chief Bad Boy, father of 'Che Washi Wobble, made the heroic self-sacrifice of offering up his own daughter to try the only maneuver that their aged Medicine Man thought would ever work. Bringing Washi and his finest marksmen silently across the bay in the dark of night to the little island off Brown's Point, he stationed each of them in favorable positions; then they all waited for the dawn. The sky began to lighten perceptibly, yet not a leaf stirred on the opposite point. The first bird of morning flew by, a fish jumped, each apparently in search of the early worm.

Yet not a leaf stirred, not even a horse turd.

Then Bad Boy beckoned to his daughter, and made suitable motions to station his men. Each took his or her place. The Big Show was about to commence. It did, and was over so fast, we have very little to relate – just four summarizing sentences. There simply wasn't anything else:
1. *'Che Washi Wobble* stepped out of the bushes
2. She walked down to the shore to bathe
3. Every Sioux immediately leapt right out of his thicket and straight up in the air, howling "BRAVO!" in Sioux
4. Ojibwe marksmen pumped every one of them full of lead before they even got back down on the ground.

Incredible, but true!

Paul never saw the last half of any of Washi's famous abdominal gyrations – belly dances – because he would start chasing her before she was halfway through. And like any decent, virtuous, demure,

Courtship of 'Che-Washi-Wobble by Paul Bunyan.

scheming, viciously deceptive, and essentially fatal Indian maiden – or indeed any normal woman regardless of race, religion, sex, politics, shoe size, or eating habits – Washi pretended to elude Paul one day by dashing into the woods. INTO THE WOODS?

And thus began one of history's greatest romances. Over hill and dale they went; and while Washi did manage to keep her cool, Paul's temperature went so high it set the woods on fire behind him. Today Highway 371 essentially lies upon what was called in those ancient times the Leech Lake Trail; and that name originated in the scorched swath cut by Paul as he chased his future bride all the way from Old Crow Wing at the confluence of the Crow Wing and Mississippi Rivers, to Agency Bay on Leech Lake.

Eventually 'Che Washi Wobble gave in and let Paul capture her – big hairy surprise! Besides, there was no place left to run to; and no Indian maiden ever backtracked.

REFERENCES

1. Coleman, B.; Frogner, E.; and Eich, E.: *Ojibwa Myths and Legends*, Ross and Haines, Inc., Minneapolis, Mn., iv + 135 (1961)
2. Landes, R.: *Ojibwa Religion and the Midewiwin*, Univ. of Wisconsin Press, Madison, Wisc., xi + 250 (1968)
3. Gringhuis, D.: *Lore of the Great Turtle – Indian Legends of Mackinac Retold*, Mackinac Island State Park Comm., Mackinac Island, Mich., vi + 89 (1970)
4. Leekly, T. B.: *The World of Manabozho: Tales of the Chippewa Indians*, Vanguard Press, Inc., New York, 128 pp (1965)
5. Clark, E. E.: *Indian Legends from the Northern Rockies*, Univ. of Oklahoma Press, Norman, Ok., xxv + 350 (1966)
6. Barnouw, V.: *Wisconsin Chippewa Myths and Tales*, Univ. of Wisconsin Press, Madison, Wisc., viii + 295 (1977)
7. Johnston, B.: *Ojibway Heritage*, Columbia Univ. Press, New York, 171 pp (1976)

LITTLE GAZONK · THE BUNYAN'S BLESSED BUNDLE

So the two were married, with the blessing of the *Mdewinini* or local Ojibwe priest; and they were feasted with suitable ceremonies. Paul then took his bride to a special place in the northern part of the State to which he had always felt a strong magnetic attraction – never dreaming that he had actually discovered what would later become the most famous deposits of iron ore in all the world – namely the Mesabi Range. This is usually attributed to the Merritt brothers, and it took seven of them to do it. The Hull-Rust-Mahoning pit just outside Hibbing today marks the place where they bedded down for that first memorable night, Paul gently scraping away the soil, rocks, boulders, hills, and glacial drift, plus the taconite and a few pre-Cambrian iron formations, to make a comfortable resting place for his beloved bride.

Also in his ever-thoughtful way, Paul carefully dumped those scrapings into Lake Superior just off the North Shore, so that in later centuries we tourists could enjoy what is properly called Isle Royale – historic landmark and relic of nothing less than the Paul Bunyan Honeymoon. This is *real* Paul Bunyan Honeymoon Country for sure, *yes ma'am!* The great iron range in that area has ever since been known as the Mesabi, in all history books as well as every geography of the world. And if anyone doubts the authenticity of this legend, go consult Father Baraga's *Dictionary of the Otchipwe Language*[1]. For *Mesabi* or "Missabay" is the Indian word for "sleeping giant" – despite the fact they did but little sleeping there that night.

Not surprisingly, some quite unusual happenings marked this marriage between Minnesota's two most unusual people, and the one a Redskin at that, while the other was a Whiteskin. First and foremost, we must remember that, as large as 'Che Washi Wobble was in comparison to other squaws, she was still far short of matching Paul. So before consenting to give

his daughter away, the venerable old *Kwiwisensish* – or Chief Big Mouth as the English called him, from the earlier French *Gros Gueule* – made Paul promise something by swearing on a wet skunk hide, something that had really never been heard of before, not even in medical journals.

Furthermore, Paul acquiesced. The gist of it all was this: It seems the great tribal Medicine Man *Kechi Ho-Ho Ragamuffin* had set out upon his usual fast and vision quest when learning of the approaching marriage of the daughter of his beloved Chief. For nothing was more important to any Indian than seeking a marriage blessing from the Spirit World. However, Kechi had first chanced upon one of the very early Minnesota logging camps while heading into the woods for his lonely vigil; and he, Ho-Ho, simply couldn't resist joining the ha-ha happy 'Jacks on their usual Sunday dessert of pickles and ice cream. The result was that Ho-Ho had some very unusual visions.

First there arose before him that night, out of the smoke of his flickering campfire, an object shaped like an apple, but with all seven orifices of the human face. Next a huge pumpkin took shape, complete with belly button, which simply rolled around the place in great glee and obvious enjoyment. Finally the famed and secret plant of Grand Medicine arose before his astonished gaze – *Ginseng!* This is the bitubercular root which carries Nature's secret imprint of the lower human torso!

To learn what this strange series of oracular appearances meant, Ragamuffin stood on his head on a big flat stone for three whole days and nights – one for each vision – while rotating slowly with the Sun daytime in order to grind in the answers. Finally he got it! Success! The Spirit World had answered *numero uno* among all potential problems presented by the prospective marriage.

For the size of a kid sired by Paul Bunyan would

Medicine Man *Kechi Ho-Ho Ragamuffin* experiencing rare visions
after a day at the logging camp.

The problem was to figure out what
the visions meant.

not only put an impossible strain on any female delivery system, but the mother might actually explode before the nine months was up. In the first place, nobody would want to mop up such a mess; second, it would louse up their whole beautiful countryside. Besides, it was Big Mouth's only daughter.

So Ho-Ho put a band-aid on the top of his head and returned to the village; and soon they all worked out an agreement that Paul and Washi would have their first kid on an *installment plan*. That is, they would divide the one kid up to get three. The first would be virtually all head, the second principally belly, while the third would specialize on the legs. Thus the birth of each would at least be practicable, even if not easy; and all of it was in fine keeping with the mighty visions of Kechi Ho-Ho Ragamuffin.

Furthermore, not only would such an arrangement bring the engineering calculations for stress and strain back into a workable obstetrics, but three such unusual boys would certainly provide endless material for campfire yarns and legends in later centuries. And this they sure did.

Apparently it never occurred to any of them at the time that one or more might come out a girl – which would be somewhat ghastly for the first arrival, utterly tragic for the mid-member, and simply too embarrassing for the last. We shall accordingly proceed to discuss the first arrival, while counting our beads for

The famed *Gazonk*, first of the three installments on the Bunyan kid, and
virtually all brain.

a right line-up of the following two, until that fateful
time when all three will have safely arrived.

GAZONK was the name the loving new parents
gave their first-born, which was happily a son,
though at that point the sequence didn't much matter. From whence the name? Well, *ga* or *ka* in Ojibwe
means "place"; and *zonk* is an old Tlingit word for
"think-tank", which Washi's brother had brought
back from a long hike to the Straits of Juan de Fuca
and the Alexander Archipelago off the Pacific Coast.
In fact, he happened to be there at the very time that
the Vikings sailed into the Pacific through the
Panama Canal, these unsung heroes beating by centuries the so-called record of Magellan who took the
longer route. Now, all the Tlingit Indians ever do is
sit around and think; and when the action-seeking
Vikings looked upon them all crouched in deep
thought, and naturally presuming they were crouched for other purposes, the lead Swede stepped up and
said:

"I tank ve go home!"

Maybe Washi's brother didn't⋅ quite get the

message, but it makes good etymology. For indeed little Gazonk proved to be *The Place of the Think-Tank*.

Quite a boy! Already at age 1 Gazonk was able to
speak both Ojibwe and Sioux; and by two he knew
every native language on the Continents of both
North and South America, from the Alaskan
Aglemiut, Macmiut, Kuskwogmiut, and Kogmiut;
down through the Tlingit, Tsimshian, Bella Coola,
Kwakiutl, and Skitswish of the northerly Pacific
Coast; back inland to the Piegan, Athapascan, Black-
foot, Shuswap, Siksika, Kawachotlin, and Cree;
through central and eastern tribes of Nugumiut,
Kigiktagmiut, Montagnais, Naskap, Ungava,
Waswanipi; also his own New England tribes of Mic-
mac, Malecite, Abnaki, Algonkin, Penobscot, Iro-
quois, Huron, and Pennakook; out to the Great
Lakes tribes of Menominee, Potawatomi, Ottawa,
Kickapoo, Fox, Sac; thence back southeasterly to the
Kaskaskia, Tamaroa, Shawnee, Tuscarora, Sus-
quehanna, Delaware, Cherokee, Muskogee, Calusa,
and Apalachee; thence the Pawnee, Ponca, Arikara,
Chickasaw, and Choctaw off to the south, with the

Though through sheer serendipity, Gazonk discovers electricity
and invents the electric light.

Navajo, Apache, Papago, Nez Percé, Comanche, Pima, and Paiute Indians in far southwest; thence down into the Aztec, Toltec, Olmec, and Mayas of Meso-America, and on into the Inca and pre-Inca of Peru.

In fact, he even went so far with the languages native to South America that he was able to converse with the penguins of Antarctica, despite the fact that he had never seen any except in the local zoo. The only languages he could never master were Brooklynese and Lumberjack jargon.

At age 3 Gazonk was picking his ears with a pair of lead pencils when a lightning bolt struck nearby and lit up the tin bucket that his mother Washi had strapped to his head to protect him from the rain. This produced the first electric light, long before Edison's time. And of course this proved that lightning was electricity, centuries before Benjamin Franklin ever rigged up his silly old kopy-kat kite.

Naturally, all these things greatly excited Gazonk's intellectual curiosity, besides giving him one helluva shock. So during that summer he wound his mother's wire clothesline into coils around a couple of granite blocks for insulators, then coupled these in turn to her big iron cookpot. When the last storm of the season hit, a bolt of lightning produced the first atomic disintegrator, which scientists today mistakenly refer to as the Van der Graaff accelerator.

The following spring, at age 4, he discovered anti-matter by using his rig to produce positrons, or anti-electrons. Carl D. Anderson in 1932, hell! Scientists today at M.I.T., Brookhaven, Berkeley, and the *Centre Européen Recherche Nucléaire* simply do not know their own antecedents.

By age 5 Gazonk was producing small atomic bombs to knock squirrels out of trees when everybody else was using bows and arrows. The trouble with this was that there was never anything left of the squirrel to eat; and besides he was making big holes in the ground which Ma was always falling into. So Paul made him stop.

Gazonk then turned to studying the strange gas that came off water when electric current from his lightning-harnesser rig went through it. The gas, of course, turned out to be hydrogen; and on his 6th Birthday he pleased his mother immensely by announcing that the reason her kitchen pans occasionally popped their enamel was that the dumb metallurgists making the steel had gotten hydrogen into it[2]. How? Well, obviously foundry heat had broken up the H_2O water molecules on damp days to give:

$$H_2O \rightarrow 2H + \frac{1}{2}O_2$$

84

$$\nabla \cdot E = \frac{\rho}{\varepsilon_o}$$

$$\nabla \times E = -\frac{\delta B}{\delta t}$$

$$x_i{}^2 + y_i{}^2 + z_i{}^2 = c^2 t_i{}^2$$

Gazonk invents mini-A-bombs to hunt squirrels.

Brother! why hadn't somebody thought of that simple thing before? Modern steelmaking has greatly benefited from this discovery, since that same gas blisters electroplate, causes boilers to explode, and wrecks airplane propellers. In the great South St. Colombo Veldt of Southern Nisswa, a Gazonk Blast Furnace today stands as his testimonial.

In his seventh year Gazonk discovered silicon monoxide by sticking a welding electrode through the bottom of an inverted flowerpot and into a pile of beach sand. The strange gaseous stuff, representing volatilized quartz with its oxygen reduced according to $C + SiO_2 \rightarrow SiO_2 + CO$, later became used for a lot of things such as coating optical lenses on cameras and telescopes. But the fish didn't like it because it also coated their fish-eye lenses.

By age 8 Gazonk began to turn his attention to the rivers, lakes, and hills around him – geology. First he invented the outboard motor, some 215 years before Johnson; and it was his great delight to put these on the wanigans to relieve the men from poling. But the fish in our Minnesota Lakes in those days were in fact and in truth the original grandfathers of our modern so-called "lunkers" – real big! They thought the buzzing motor was an unusually fine lunker-size fly, whereupon they snapped them up as fast as

Gazonk could mount them on the wanigans. So he finally gave it all up; but for years after, no 'Jack ever dared sleep on a wanigan, or even close to the waterfront of any of our larger lakes – not if he snored. For the lunkers might think he was a motorized fly.

In the field of geology itself, Gazonk came up with an astonishing discovery: That there was indeed a Great Flood, much as preserved in the legends from both sides of his family; that it happened the same time and from the same causes as the Great Ice Age; and that both resulted in a rather natural manner from enormous volcanic action taking place beneath the Atlantic Ocean. Many centuries later scientists would discover that the greatest mountain range in the world not only lies beneath the Atlantic Ocean, but that it is entirely built of lava that poured through the crust beneath. They would even find that so much seawater had evaporated during each Great Ice Age as to cause the ocean levels all over the world to drop some 30 peavey poles, or approximately a city block. But this was so far ahead of his time that it's still ahead of ours. Oh you Gazonk!

When he was 9, and finding that nobody was aroused by likening the boiling off of ocean water to his mother's teakettle, Gazonk turned to Einstein's theory for time and space. GREAT WEASEL

That fateful event which led to the world's greatest
invention – the "Gazonker" which makes oysters
shuck themselves and willingly.

GUTS! The old bearded coot that his father bragged
about so much was off by a full mile! His equations:

$$x' = \boldsymbol{\gamma}\,(x - vt) \quad ; \quad y' = y$$
$$t' = \boldsymbol{\gamma}\,(t - vx/c^2) \qquad z' = z$$
$$\boldsymbol{\gamma} = (1 - v^2/c^2)^{-\frac{1}{2}}$$

should never have that dumb $(1 - v^2/c^2)^{-\frac{1}{2}}$ in the
denominator! For this meant a miscalculation by
years if anybody tried visiting other worlds at some
good fraction of the speed of light! Yet, who cared?
So Gazonk simply sat back and decided to let future
generations stew in their own juices. They should
have listened to him.

Then at age 10 it happened: *The Great Achieve-
ment!* Gazonk's Dad and Ma *loved* to eat clams – and
oysters whenever travelers brought them from the
east. But they ate so many that it was a real drag getting the dam things shucked. There must be an easier
and quicker way.

About that time an old friend of Paul's from Kennebunkport visited them in a Model T Ford carrying
a trunk filled with choice oysters. Examining the
motor one day with his usual intense curiosity,
Gazonk happened to have one hand on the old
Model T spark coil just as he was pushing the ignition button with the other –

Ho-Ho! HEE!! WHOOEY WOWWOW!!!

40,000 volts! So *that's* how they did it! His single hair
stood straight on end; his ears wobbled and even
began to smoke; and for that one brief instant
Gazonk didn't much care about anything except getting the cry-eye out of there – but fast!

As he sat under a tree trying to regain his senses,
the young genius happened to think about the
oysters in the trunk. Why, those miserable little juicy
critters and their annoying habit which simply burned him up: They would hang onto their shells come
Hades or High Water. Nothing else seemed to be on
their little cotton-pickin' minds except to avoid being
slooped. Weird attitude, really.

BUT – what if they went through the experience
he just had? If the 40,000-volt shock even made him
forget Einstein for awhile, why wouldn't an oyster
forget to hang on to his shell?

In fact, wouldn't an oyster experience Gazonk's
own reaction in trying to get the hell out of there –
but *fast*? Certainly their comfortable little home
would immediately become the first place *not* to be,
and with top priority.

Maybe he could even get those stubborn little critters *to shuck themselves*!!??

And thus was born little Gazonk's famous
OYSTER SHOCKER, I mean *shucker*.

REFERENCES

1. Baraga, (Bishop): *A Dictionary of the Otchipwe Language, Explained in English*, Orig. pub. 1878; Ross & Haines, Inc., Minneapolis, Mn., Part I: English-Otchipwe, 301 pp; Part II: Otchipwe-English, viii + 422 (1966)
2. With vast self-restraint compensating for a natural lack of modesty, a dozen or more references to scientific publications of the author are

omitted in this section. The excuse for this autobiographic imposi-
tion is that it confers credulity upon Gazonk's prowess by running in
a few facts which are about as weird as fiction, taken from the real life
of a weird character. The stuff for the most part is legit – for the most
part.

CHAPTER IX

THE GAZONK
OYSTER SHUCKER

With a fierce cunning unlike the mild-mannered little guy that he was, and with a glint of expectant satisfaction in each eye, Gazonk opened the trunk and took out that first fat oyster which, completely unknown to itself, would become one of this world's greatest pioneers.

Then he ran a pair of lead wires from the two poles of the shock coil; he placed the totally unsuspecting oyster on a copper plate attached to one of the leads; next he gently touched the other to the top of his wet shell.

Then he turned on the ignition:

POWWGH!

IT WORKED!

Not only did the shell pop open, but J. P. Oyster got out so fast it nearly went into orbit!

To test the perfection of his exciting and quite astonishing invention, and showing that he was indeed the greatest scientist in the history of logging, Gazonk tied the leads to a few more. No question about it: *He had struck oil!*

To make the thing perfectly dazzling, Gazonk tested out the distance of jump; and he found to his inexpressible satisfaction that, for any given voltage above some threshold value V_t, all oysters jumped the same distance. For the full coil at 40,000 volts, they went an even 13.00 feet. With the coil shunted to produce only 30,000 volts, it was exactly 9 feet 6 inches. Shunting further to 20,000 sent them 3 feet 8 inches; at 15,000 volts the oyster would open his shell, but not jump; and at 10,000 volts the hardy critters simply shook a little, giggled rather audibly inside their shells, and stayed put.

So Gazonk went back to the full 40,000, since his huge parents would need the whole 13-foot clearance; and he then invited them to his special surprise party.

First they were fitted with blindfolds, next led to a comfortable spot beneath a tree near the car. He bade them lie down, facing his invention – though they knew nothing of it at the time; and then with filial love and devotion, he propped up each of their

That historic event – captured at the very moment – of **THE WORLD'S FIRST OYSTER WHICH SHUCKED ITSELF!!!**

heads with a pillow – and had them open their mouths.

Back at the firing platform, Gazonk had meantime arranged a chute leading from the supply trunk placed on a stepladder, so that the oysters would drop

Gazonk treats his beloved parents to a feast of self-shucking oysters.

one by one onto the copper plate placed just 13 feet from his parents' mouths. On went the ignition. *Pop!* went an oyster. The aim was perfect for Dad. A swivel beneath the plate allowed him to rotate it slightly by pulling a rope. Another *pop!* And Ma had a particularly juicy one right between the teeth.

Words would fail to express the joy of Mr. and Mrs. P. Bunyan as they found their first choice among all juicy morsels splashing down on their palates almost as fast as they could slide the last one down the hatch; and even with the beating of drums and shooting of fireworks we could never fully convey their sense of astonishment. It was simply a great day, and not just for the proud parents. It was a *gr-ea-t d-a-y* for oyster lovers all over the world!

For when word got back to Oyster Country on the Atlantic Coast, and particularly such places as Long Island Sound and Chesapeake Bay, the excitement became indescribable. Every Model T Ford was promptly dismantled on sight, such that highway traffic virtually vanished. For any oyster addict would sooner eat than travel. Nobody spoke of oyster *shucking* any more, but only of oyster *shocking*.

Understandably, research scientists from both large and small oceanographic institutions soon got into the act. One of the first things they discovered was the reason behind the peculiar problem with smaller oysters, which at times failed to jump. However, not until the Psychology Department at Columbia University started their studies was the reason fully explained. For these able men, and women, found that the oyster has a memory function

Discovery of the NSE (North-South Effect) during a game with "Gazonkers" at the One Shot Saloon.

of sorts, by which it reduces experiential reactions to the autonomous nervous system much as in higher animals. Thus an oyster less than a year old, who has not yet gone through the full four seasons, and hence finds everything new anyway, tends simply to take the electric shock as another of the odd-ball features of life on this planet, whereupon he stays in his shell.

On the other hand, and to the very marked contrary, the older oyster has the feeling he "knows it all" after reaching his first birthday or so; and when that old Model T Ford shock coil goes into action, he's had it. You simply cannot teach an old oyster new tricks. He just doesn't want to hang around, waiting to prove it all out by still another experience, nor even to ask questions.

At one of the more sophisticated oceanographic institutes on Maryland's Eastern Shore, an oldtime waterman came in one day with the observation of what later became known as the North-South Effect. He and his buddies at the One Shot Saloon had developed a game in which they took the brass "gaboons", which were still around from old times for those who chewed tobacco, and arranged these in a circle so that a number of players could sit inside a central ring, then compete for accuracy of their shocking, or shucking.

Rapidly mounting evidence showed that men with

their gaboons aligned generally N-S were consistently scoring higher than those having them aligned E-W. In fact, the situation was getting so bad it was leading to brawls over choice of position. The scientists soon found they had something there, yes indeed.

For inside each oyster a tiny wad of magnetically reacting protein was discovered, attached to the ligament which causes crawl. Nobody had ever paid any attention before to how, where, or why oysters move when they move; but this is apparently the control mechanism which helps them know their direction, much like migrating birds. Under natural conditions the oyster has time to use his magnetic impulse as a direction-finder, which is then followed by a reaction of choice as to where he wants to go.

However, prompted by Gazonk's shock coil, there is no time for the second action of choice as to where to go. He simply goes, and the faster the better. So the direction is usually either forward to the north, or backward to the south.

Very shortly after this intriguing discovery, it was put to tremendous commercial advantage – and fortunately so, in view of the vast upsurge in the oyster market. First, some smart guys rigged a chute of rather mild inclination, so as not to cause the oyster to grow thin from overworking; and they placed this chute to lead from the oyster beds out in the Bay to

Magnetically controlled oysters delivering themselves for self-shucking at Tilghman's Island on Maryland's Eastern Shore.

the oyster house on shore. Attached to the chute's underside was a row of cobalt-nickel magnets, oriented north-south and placed progressively up the chute.

RESULT: The whole bed would go in slow but orderly migration, crawling up the chute and delivering themselves – to the great relief of the tongers who had always done it the hard way before.

In fact, this seemed to mark the end of all possible invention. For the oysters now not only shucked themselves, but delivered themselves to market.

CHAPTER X

GAZONK'S FLYING CLAMS
and the
ARRIVAL OF BROTHER
BULLY BELLY B'HOY

MEANTIME BACK ON THE MISSISSIPPI Gazonk was doing no sleeping at the switch – neither were Paul and 'Che Washi Wobble. On the one hand, it was fast coming time for the arrival of a little brother – well, little by comparison with moose, dinosaurs, and the two parents. We refer, of course, to the second installment on the Bunyan Kid, who would hopefully show up as one they could name Bully Belly B'Hoy.

But it was touch and go, with all hands on deck each day manning the prayer wheels. Washi had something on the way, alright; that was most evident. In fact, she was casting so much shadow that half the people in her tribe were turning white for lack of sunshine.

We won't record the legend concerning her morning sickness, which began about the 35th month – it took some four years to gestate each of these oversized odd-ball kids. Suffice it to say that oldtimers have an explanation of their own for the Grand Canyon.

On the other hand, there was *Kechi-Gazonk* as the Ojibwe now called him, their *Kechi* meaning "great", as seen in Longfellow's *Gitchi Gumi* for *Kechi-gami* or Great Water, and as indeed appears in "Mississippi" itself, where the *Missi-* is mere local dialect for *mechi*, and identical with *kechi*, while the *-sippi* is the Ojibwe *sebe* for "river" – hence Great River. Got it? You still there?

Now, this Great River was loaded with an oyster-like critter called *ess* by the Indians, but "clam" by Paul who knew them from the lakes of Maine. That delicious trunkful of Chincoteagues originally brought west by their lumberjack friend in his old Model T, of course, was long since gone; and none was available for replacement – not in Minnesota. But there were sure plenty of clams; and although Indians in general regard the clam as one of the lowest forms of food – for unknown reasons – Gazonk's temptation to try his oyster shucker on clams was

Gazonk discovers the strange Ferromagnetic Effect in Minnesota clams.

naturally irresistible.

So Gazonk soon had himself set up to lob a few choice river clams into Daddy's big gub. First he had Pop stretch out beneath the tree as usual; but this time he couldn't invite Ma because her pod stuck up

Babe the Blue Ox helps deliver **Bully Belly
B'hoy,** second installment on the Bunyan
kid.

so high he was unable to get enough lift into his shot
to clear the obstacle.

However, even with Dad properly placed, a problem developed which Gazonk had not anticipated. This was Iron Country, we will recall, home of some of the world's greatest mines of the future, as we had earlier mentioned in discussing the Bunyan Honeymoon. The rich ore was heavily doused with the ferromagnetic oxide Fe_3O_4, instead of the usual paramagnetic sesquioxide Fe_2O_3. Surveyors had always been plagued by this, their compasses dancing wildly, and typically pointing in some odd-ball direction having but little relation to the true planetary North Pole.

And so it was that, when Gazonk pushed the button to electrocute a Mississippi river clam, instead of following the usually carefully planned $h = \frac{1}{2}gt^2$ trajectory into Dad's mouth, where h is the elevation, g the gravitational constant, and t the time in flight, the dog-boned critter took off in spirals and giddy dances that were impossible to control, and which completely ruined his aim.

One clam even came back and hit Gazonk in the eye! This was a bit much.

However, the mystery was solved a few weeks later when a runner from the East Coast reported the discovery of the magnetic protein in oysters. Gazonk immediately cut up a clam and found that, in Iron Country, this little ferruginous gland of the oyster is vastly augmented in the clam. Hence the direction of clam travel in the sand is not only magnetically directed, but even when it is in flight. He really

should have known this without being told; for every kid growing up in the Lake Region is acquainted with the fact that clam tracks on sandy lake bottoms *always* run N-S except over iron ore deposits; and many a kid has left a toy containing some magnetic part on the beach overnight, only to find it buried beneath a pile of clams in the morning.

Another strange and interesting thing about clams, Gazonk found, was that their voltage-reaction characteristics were quite different from those of oysters. In the first place, the clam was more rugged, sluggish, and generally stupid, such that voltages had to be higher to accomplish the same results. For example, no clam even giggles at 10,000 volts; and to lift them out of the shell requires that they be at least two years old, rather than one for the oyster. The reason for this proved to rest with the Minnesota winter. Any clam recovering from the shock of his first Minnesota winter simply used the 40,000 volts to warm up.

About the time Gazonk was adding extra wire to his coil, stepping the voltage into the 50,000 – 60,000 range where he really got a reaction, Ma Washi began nearing delivery time. The scene soon became positively horrendous, and it was all hands on deck. When she went into labor at dawn on St. Valentine's Day, seismographs in Alaska registered 7.1 on the open-ended Richter Scale. In nearby Nebraska, shock waves from the pounding and hollering sent even the bravest Kiowa and Arapahoe warriors head-over-heels into the woods along with, and soon far ahead of, their women and children. It was every man for himself. Passing west over the Rockies muffled the waves just enough so that both the Apaches and Nez Percé's thought the Omahas, Arikaras, Kiowas, Blackfeet, and Shoshoni had banded together to go on the warpath against them, and that they would soon be seen charging over the mountains.

Realizing that nothing but extinction could result for a single tribe coming up against such a huge host, these two ancient and inveterate enemies immediately signed an irrevocable blood contract of alliance – then headed for the opposite hills hoping to overtake their women and children.

When the hour for delivery arrived, so did the problem of what to do with a kid who was all belly. The Chief's aged grandmother was called in as midwife, because it was generally believed she had seen everything. But when she looked upon Bully Belly B'Hoy starting to stick his small head out of the original model for the Texas Astrodome, she realized she hadn't seen nothing yet.

None less than Bully's lumberjack father saved the day – yes, our Grand Old Man Paul Bunyan himself. Quietly greasing up the runners on the old logging sled, used years before to haul his belongings west from Maine, Paul hitched his dear Babe the Blue Ox to the front end, then pushed the rear of the sled through the flap on the wigwam to the rapidly panicking corps of midwives – yes, there were now five of them, four more having been brought in as emergency helpers from neighboring tribes. Paul reasoned that, if you could skid logs, you could skid a kid. And the panicky perspiring squaws were glad to welcome his help.

In moments the natural sequence transpired, and out came Bully Belly and all, right on the skidwagon. A perfect shot! The great Blue Ox leaned forward, strained a mighty strain. Slowly the skid slid with the kid. A new Bunyan was born! Or at least the second of three installments.

For a moment, however, it was touch-and-go. The problem: How to slap a kid on the butt to start inhalation when for all practical purposes he had no butt? For the butt installment would not arrive until some unknown future date when it would be specifically featured by Beautiful Legs Benson.

Fortunately – or unfortunately, depending on what side of the Rockies one views the situation – a squaw named *Kechi Mittquay* or Big-Fisted Woman simply took it upon herself to swing a real haymaker right on the kid's pod.

This did it, and all was well – here. The kid let out a snort, and his lungs took off. But over the mountains it was trouble all over again, and this time for real. While the Apaches and Nez Percé's were each rushing to their respective villages to grab their belongings and flee from the wrath to come, the resonating *BWONGGG – BWONGGG – BWONGGG* coming over the mountains from Bully Belly B'Hoy's belly now echoed back from their own hills. In their already excited state, each thought the other had broken contract and were sounding their tom-toms for war.

So they furiously rushed into a scalping orgy which would have brought complete annihilation of male members in both tribes if the women hadn't happily intervened. It seems that during their flight to the hills, the earlier earth-shaking ruckus had continued to echo between Rockies and Sierra Nevadas, losing hundreds of decibels in intensity during each pass back and forth. Finally on the seventeenth echo these dear women began to recognize the noise as coming from one of their own kind, going through an experience they all knew well – though certainly it was unusually loud.

SO-O-O-O – we have now brought the story of our great folk hero Paul Bunya(r)n through countless joys, trials, tribulations, and celebrations, to the point where he has a family of four – or two and two-thirds depending on how you look at it – with his adorable but somewhat massive squaw 'Che Washi Wobble bringing him two fine sons – or two-thirds of a son, depending on how hung up you may be on physiology.

In any event, the story now returns to Big Brother, the inimitable Gazonk. For the arrival of Bully Belly B'Hoy immediately put a great strain on both ends of the Bunyan commissary – intake and output, food and diapers, ingestion and exgestion, infecation and defecation, and so on. After all, this child was all belly, and of Bunyanesque proportions.

At first Gazonk stepped up to offer a supply of his shucked (er, oops! *shocked*) clams, with the idea that the slippery things would slide down the esophageal tube faster, helping fill him to the mark on his tank where howling stops and sleep begins. In fact, they had to wean Bully very early. His head, we will recall, was very small because most of it was on Gazonk's shoulders. So his mouth had a bad fit for Washi's faucet. This would get her all upset, such that through sheer eagerness she often shot him right in the eye. Far better for mother to get "milk leg" than for son to get "milk eye".

But a more urgent situation developed over the emergent end. Indeed, this is where our word "emergency" comes from. Such an immense food factory going into operation threw every fly in Minnesota into ecstacies of delight. They simply couldn't wait to collect around the Bunyan Dispos-all, namely the two-story three-holer out back, where the men got to sit on the second level until the ERA stepped in; and they also enjoyed flying around the wigwam itself – and much more annoyingly, around Bully himself. Then they would rush back to their own fly wigwams and shack up for the next production. Maggots became so plentiful that the competition made them learn to eat wood, and finally solid rock. The situation reached the extreme where Paul couldn't even find his wigwam one day, it was so covered with flies; and when he finally recognized it and hollered: "SHOO!", the flies naturally all tried to take off at once. But you can't do this if there is not enough wing room; and when they dug in their feet for purchase and jumped, the wigwam went with them. Fortunately it dropped only a few miles away when enough of the flies lost their footings.

So the Bunyans had a really serious fly situation, and Gazonk decided to do something about it. Again his research methods were quite unusual, indeed to a

Paul Bunyan's Dispos-all, later copied by Chic Sales, where men got the second story until the days of OSHA, the ERA, and the Society for Battered Wives.

Gazonk learning clam language at a depth of 3 meters.

then turned away in disgust and took another route. But that route was also blocked, by another clam. Gazonk heard a distinct: "*Pssst!*" as this second clam tried to signal that the traveler's way was blocked; and there was a grating response: "*Grrr!*" just before this second clam – which was much smaller than the first – decided to get out of the way of the first clam.

To shorten a long story for present purposes, Gazonk discovered that (a) clams definitely are conversationalists among themselves, (b) their vocabulary as might be expected is limited to eating and elementary experiences while crawling, and (c) they don't have any vowels – just consonants. Apparently to pronounce a vowel, one must purse his lips; and clams don't have any. Again, a clam can make consonantal noises just by grinding his shells together, whereas a vowel would require blowing a bubble. Clams rarely own a bubble to blow. In fact, it has always been a puzzling thing to hear a clam called a "bivalve", since it doesn't appear to have any valve at all; and one now wonders whether this might be just a dialectical distortion of 'bye-vowel, meaning to use consonants only, and bye-bye vowels.

In any event, here are some typical clam conversations with translations as recorded by Gazonk:

1. "Hmm Bd, wtz gnw?"
   (Hi, Bud, what's new?)
2. "Zhw gt lk t klc fml wt jst crwld b?"
   (You got a look at the classy female what just crawled by?)
3. "Mv vr bfr r slp w n kssr!"
   (Move over before I slap you on the kisser!)

Within a few weeks Gazonk learned how to talk back at them by grinding his teeth on a clam shell, holding a small rock in each cheek to make the clicking sounds they use for punctuation, and sliding his tongue in and out at various angles in imitation of their much-used body language. His first conversation turned up the interesting information that the clams had had an unusually tough winter, food was still scarce, and they were hungry. Gazonk asked them what they ate. They replied they ate the bodies of dead insects that drowned overhead and drifted down to the bottom. Gazonk said:

"Hw lk mm-mm frsh nd lv?" (How would you like to eat them fresh and live?) Now the clam, of course, can't say "eat" because there are too many vowels; but it can convey the idea of a delicious repast by the consonants mm-mm.

To this the clams replied: "Hw?" or how? Whereupon Gazonk said he would teach them to fly.

Naturally, this strained their imagination as well as their vocabulary; and he was underwater until sunset before he could really develop any satisfactory clam-idea of his perfectly brilliant plan. The main thrust was threefold: First, they must trust him implicitly, even to his taking them out of their water habitat and laying them on his launch plate; second, when they felt an almost irresistible – he would hold the voltage down a bit – urge to leap out of their shell, they must fight to hold onto it and bring it with them; and third, once they found themselves airborne, they must learn to fly, just like humans have to learn to swim when visiting clams. After all, their two big shells made a natural for flapping and getting into flight.

point of having no precedent in world history. The only exception to that statement might be the work of the U.S. Navy's Oceanographic crews assigned to researching possibilities of intelligent communication between man and porpoises, or killer whales, by using their own mammalian language. But clams ain't mammals. Nobody would ever dare suggest the possibility of talking to a clam.

Nobody except Gazonk, that is. His hearing, of course, was exceptionally keen, since his peculiar development maximized and optimized everything in the head. And Gazonk thought he had heard one particularly fat and large old clam make a few derogatory remarks one day when the spark coil failed to open his shell.

Knowing that water is an excellent medium for transmitting sound, and being convinced that the best way to get to know any critter is to study it in its native habitat, Gazonk outfitted himself with a few oxygen tanks and other scuba equipment, then spent every Wednesday afternoon lying quietly on some lake bottom while listening to clam talk. He had heard some of the old Indian wise men occasionally use the expression: "Clam up!" instead of: "Shut up!"; and this further convinced him that such a research had real possibilities. For if a clam is able to "clam up" just like people "shut up", then the clam must also have been doing some talking, or there would be nothing to clam up from.

One day it definitely happened: A clam inching toward him on the bottom sands suddenly *grunted*,

94

Gazonk's "flying clams" cleaning up the fly
situation around Bully Belly B'hoy's tub of used diapers.

In those days, as even schoolchildren know, to say
nothing of grieving ornithologists, our lands were
literally covered with the glorious and delicious bird
known as the *passenger pigeon*. They filled our skies in
feathery clouds; and many a pioneer, lost in the
woods and threatened with starvation, had his life
saved by the simple expedient of knocking a pigeon
meal off the low branches of some tree, using a mere
stick.

Then came Gazonk's Flying Clams. They dined
like kings – and grew and grew. In less time than it
takes to tell the sad story, every passenger pigeon in
America was gone. The species became extinct.

What next? By now these frightening calcareous-
winged monsters were of pterodactyl size; and their
numbers were so horrendous that their burial
grounds became those spectacular limestone cliffs
which line the shores of the upper Mississippi today.
From pigeons they went to high-jumping jack-
rabbits. Soon even the deer and mountain goats got
picked off; and then the time actually came when
they started after buffalo calves, next the cows and
bulls, by sweeping low and opening wide. They loved
the buffalos because their curly hair tickled all the
way down.

And once again a complete species of our wildlife
nearly became extinct. Historians tend to blame the
disappearance of the buffalo on the rifles of the

Gazonk then brought the story to its climax so far
as both parties were concerned: They'd chase the in-
numerable juicy fresh flies, clam up when getting
one, then quickly wrap their sticky tongue around it
and head for the next one. When full: Just fall into
the lake, and their friend Gazonk would bring them
back the next day.

"Beautiful" scarcely describes what happened. The
clams simply loved it; Gazonk loved it; and Bully Belly B'Hoy was soon free of flies, which made everybody else love it. Gazonk even used the old magnet
trick to lead the clams up a chute to his launch deck
so he wouldn't have to go get them each day.

Strange and totally unforeseen, on the other hand,
was one of the consequences of this forcing of muta-
tions upon Mother Nature. For those Flying Clams
became so enamored with their liberation from the
drudgeries and drab experiences of scraping rotted
bugs and other debris off river and lake bottoms, that
they were loathe to return when the flies ran out.

Furthermore, they were now growing to quite
enormous size on the wholesome diet combined with
exercise so totally extraordinary in molluscoid life.
Soon they were attacking cicadas, dragonflies, large
moths, and butterflies. Any grasshopper taking too
high a jump became Clam Chowder – for the clam,
that is. Then the larger ones began picking off small
birds.

One of Gazonk's mutants, the horrifying
Great Flying Clam, chasing down a buffalo
dinner.

Mesabi Magnetic clams, with pearls!

Whiteman, in the hands of Reds and Whites alike; but those who write our history books were obviously never there when the hoards of Gazonk's Flying Clams swooped down out of the skies. Those that were, never returned to tell the story. For some FC's weren't too choosey!

At that point in history, Gazonk's Great Flying Clams fortunately took off for the far west. With most buffalo cleared off the prairies, and not being able to attack prey in the woods, there was nothing left for them but the wide open spaces of the Pacific Ocean. We have no record of what they did next, nor where they actually went. But there are two indications of an eventual return to marine living: First, it is known that man-eating clams exist deep in the ocean, and notably in areas near the Phillipines.

Second is the strange and sobering fact that Save-the-Whale organizations have since sprung up all over the world. There seems to be hard evidence that even this largest of all the world's animate species has been threatened with extinction. The blame is usually placed upon Japanese fishermen and professional whalers. Maybe yes; maybe no.

Might it not be that this is instead merely the climax of the vast destructive acts of Gazonk's runaway mollusk mutation, the *Great Flying Clams?*

* * * * *

Finally, we would be greatly remiss if we were to omit from this part of the narration, dealing with Gazonk's self-shucking oysters and clams, the historic Pennsylvania legend of BIGG BUCK\$.

It seems that there was a raw-boned farm lad from Dutch country north of Lebanon, Pa., named Buck Biggs. Hearing of all the commotion about logging in Minnesota, and knowing of Embryo Gelb's *(alias Johnny Appleseed's)* long lane of luscious fruit trees leading straight to the place, Buck went there and got a job as team flunkey in the sprawling Weyerhaeuser Camp north of Cohasset, Mn. Buck's job was to keep the horse-power at full throttle in days when it was

Go-go girl in a logging camp? Or just imagination?

hay and harness rather than gasoline; and he had supposed that life in a lumber camp was not much different from "down at the farm". It proved a bit different, particularly with no Paw to holler him home at the end of the day, and a Maw to stuff him with grits and head cheese, then send him to bed while she washed his stinking socks. But Buck was made of the right stuff; and to prove he didn't mind it when the going got tough, he even offered to take over the hind ends of the horses and leave the other fussy flunkey with the fronts.

So it was strictly Buck's problem when the Old Grey Mare, pulling left-center on the log hauler, threw a shoe off her right-rear hoof while crossing the Big Fish Hook just south of the Gunflint. Buck was prepared: He hauled out the Co-Ni-Mn-Cr-C magnet used for straightening compass needles when they got bent crossing the Iron Range, tied a rope around the neck of the drag horse, then threw the magnet in the river so it would be pulled along the line of team travel.

Clank! Clank! It was Bingo Day on the Big Fish Hook, and friend Buck had just struck oil. But when he reeled it in, to his combined chagrin and astonishment there was no horseshoe. Instead, both poles of the magnet were packed with river clams – great big juicy ones. In fact, they were not only choice-looking

specimens, but upon listening closely one could hear them chirping like a bunch of happy crickets, smothered under a rug and in process of eating their way through. And it was right here and now that there arose the famous old saying: "Happy as a clam!"

Because the clams looked so fat and sassy, Buck cracked one open to consider the possibility of enjoying a classy *hors d'oeuvres* before lunch. Instead, however, his attention was immediately arrested by spotting a beautiful big pearl, a real knockout. So he opened another clam: Another pearl. In fact, every dam clam had one. He had really struck it rich!

Buck quickly and correctly reasoned that the pearls had grown as usual upon irritation centers produced by ingesting a rough grain of sand; but it took him a little longer to discover that the grain in this case was the black magnetic iron oxide Fe_3O_4 characterizing the Iron Range. Since he had heard of Gazonk Bunyan's work with electromagnetic fields and oysters that were taught to shuck themselves, he probably should have recognized the similar situation earlier. But that only happened the following evening when he spread his haul all over the top of the deacon's seat back at camp. The 'Jacks were gathered around and uttering such yells of astonishment that one of the men, in process of hanging up his gear, ran in the

97

door with the magnet still in his hind pocket. Instantaneously, every pearl flew through the air and stuck to his pants. He looked like a Las Vegas go-go girl – at least in parts.

Naturally, the upshot of this story was that Buck dragged every river of the Iron Range, pulled out every clam with a pearl, and soon became so filthy rich he simply couldn't stand the sight of any more of the green stuff. Besides, his teacher at the little red schoolhouse outside Lebanon had never taught him to count beyond 999,999,999,999. He just didn't know what came next, and that made him afraid of it. So he changed his name from Buck Biggs to Bigg Buck$ and retired.

However, when taxes and inflation began eating away at his capital, clipping a few of the last nines off his bank account so that the 999,999,999,999 became only 999,999,999,888, Buck$ did go so far as to ship a load of magnetite sand from the Mesabi Iron Range to his production farm on the Youghiogheny. For a freshwater clam does not have the natural biomagnet characterizing the saltwater oyster, and the Bunyan Patent on Conveyor Belt Tonging therefore cannot be used.

But Buck$ developed an even better deal: He sprinkled magnetite on the big sandbar in the riverbend below his barn, waited a few months for the clams to get irritated guts, then pulled the magnetic wire out of his wire recorder and rigged it from sandbar to shucking barn. By keeping the wire carefully greased, he not only pulled all the pearl-pregnant clams out of the Youghiogheny, but they slid along the wire right up the hill and into his shucking tubs.

And if there is any more to this Buck Biggs and his Bigg Buck$ story, we have done our best to try to forget it.

CHAPTER XI

BEAUTIFUL LEGS BENSON AND
BUNYAN FAMILY LIFE

'Che Washi Wobble was still only 121 years old when she produced Beautiful Legs Benson. But it was wearing her out; and so far as we know, she and Paul both gave up after bringing him aboard, taking the vows of monastic life so that it would never happen again. It's just as well. For there could only be one BCG-BBB-BLB; and they (?) were all here now. Put together, they made an unforgettable sight.

The arrival of Beautiful Legs was in this wise: Ma Bunyan not only began having cramps, but the kid's kicking ran up another Richter 6.5 and almost restarted the Apache/Nez Percé war on the other side of the Rockies. Beautiful Legs, however, not only needed no slap on the butt: He came out running! In fact, Dad Paul had to be called in to hitch up Babe, lasso him, and bring him back home.

Most of the rest of Benson's story is along the same line – always running. In fact, he developed a bad sinus problem because his constant impulse to run began to extend to his nose.

When Beautiful Legs was still just a kid, his favorite pastime of outrunning elk, antelope, and deer finally came near killing the darn things off. To this day there are neither elk nor antelope in Minnesota, though both zoologists and historians know there used to be many. Beautiful Legs never fired a gun in his life; but he either chased them all the way to Alaska, or wore them out so badly they laid down and died.

Since he got his biggest kick out of racing the fastest ones, it was the elk and antelope that became locally extinct first. Then something happened that most of our modern conservationists seem to have forgotten – if they ever knew: Beautiful Legs Benson caused the founding of the Great Society of Game Wardens.

For the Indians as well as the pioneers were getting much upset about Benson's knocking off all the elk and antelope; and now he was beginning on the deer. To the Indians, this was a matter of life and death from standpoints of food supply; also, White pioneers were no longer able to talk their sweethearts into coming out in the woods to live with them because of the homungous stench of pooped-out animals.

So every resident of Northwest Territory – as it was called in those days – gathered to appoint a Game Warden. This historic first officer in the annals of Ecology, Sports Afield, the S.P.C.A., and W.C.T.U. was Warden Gordon; and the first thing Warden Gordon did was to get right out on the prairies of Todd County where Beautiful Legs was doing his running those days. None less than 45 deer shortly came streaking by – yes, streaking, for none of our Minnesota *dears* ever wears clothes; and it was obvious from their glazed eyes, perspiration-soaked fur,

Unusual birth of **Beautiful Legs Benson** –
he came out running!

Stroboscopic photo at 1.0 nano-second showing Beautiful Legs Benson about to bite the bullet fired at him by Warden Gordon.

and tongues dragging on the ground that Benson was close behind. He was. Warden Gordon hollered:

"Halt! You're under arrest!"

But Beautiful Legs was going by at Mach 3.1, so the sound never caught up with him. He never knew he had even been hollered at, let alone arrested.

Warden Gordon, immediately perceiving the great advantage of getting Beautiful Legs on a triple count of poaching, resisting arrest, and fleeing from the scene of his crime – he'd be able to lock him up for a very peaceful ten years at least – raised his .30/.30 and fired a warning shot, aimed at whistling just past Benson's ears.

However, even with its muzzle velocity of 3320 fps, that cartridge was only moving at Mach 3.2. This was just enough to catch up with the great runner, and not much more. Benson looked up, saw the bullet slowly passing him, reached out and grabbed it, put it in his mouth, bit it in two, and spit the two halves to either side, right into the herd he was running. This is where the historic expression "bite the bullet" originated. Each half-bullet then killed a deer. When the villagers later came over to Todd County to see how the Warden was doing, they saw the two dead deer, each with a chunk of lead from a .30/.30 in it; and when they put the two together, their ballistics expert proved that they were from the

Warden's gun!

So they arrested Warden Gordon himself for poaching, and threw him in jail for a very peaceful ten years – peaceful for Beautiful Legs Benson, that is, who just kept running, and running, and running.

Beautiful Legs Benson never got married, probably for two reasons: First, since he was constantly running, there was always the possibility he was running around with other women. Second, he rarely ever got a girl to the stage of a first kiss because it was so embarrassing for her to try to find his lips.

Life for the other members of the Bunyan family, of course, continued highly eventful, and always so, building legend wherever they went. Bully Belly, for example, became the origin of every tale of big appetites to come out of American logging history. Until he grew old enough to find food sources for himself, he was the main drain on Bunyan resources. To invite him as a guest for dinner was to bring disaster on the house. When in his early 'teens, and his stomach was really rounding out, Paul had to move the whole family down in the valley to keep Bully Belly B'Hoy from rolling downhill after dinner.

B'Hoy's favorite main course, of course, was beef; and he liked it raw – just pass a match sufficiently near a live steer to smell the hair. Paul had to hire a whole platoon of ranchhands, who would run in clean, then leave the pile in the doorway just before Beautiful legs came tearing by to grab his chow. Like Bully Belly slooping his soup, the same Venturi effect pulled all Ma's trash out the door and spread it throughout the woods.

By this time, incidentally, the Bunyans had given up the simple tribal accommodations and lifestyle of 'Che Washi Wobble's people. The wigwam couldn't take her constant scrubbing down the walls. So Paul built them a fine big log house. Unfortunately, however, Washi's continual washing and scrubbing soon wore the pine logs down so thin they found themselves living in a frame house; and while this had some historic value for being the first of its kind in the North Woods, the first big storm of the summer blew it away.

Paul then built a new one out of birch logs. But when Washi wore off the wood, they were left with a birchback *wigiwami* just as before.

Everybody remarks about the peculiarity of the American Indian in always wanting to wear a blanket, but nobody ever explains how it all began. Actually, the syndrome only dates back to the middle of the last century, when the Winnebagoes of Wisconsin were moved west across the Mississippi, then north to a reservation between the Long Prairie and Crow Wing Rivers, and just west of the Mississippi. Lumbering by then had begun on the St. Croix not far to the southeast where, as we will

When Bully Belly B'hoy ate too much he would often roll down the hill.

cow-bull pairs the beginning of each month, to number thirty for April, June, September, November; thirty-one for each of the other months except February, which only got twenty-eight, except for twenty-nine in Leap Year. Bully Belly, not carrying his cooking beyond said striking a match, and not having the least intention ever to milk a cow, simply ate the bull while it was still kicking, and washed it down with the whole cow.

Soup was his prime fare as an opener – lots of it and *hot*. Pa got an old iron pot of huge dimensions from the Indians – the one the Leech Lake *Mukundwa* or Pillagers used for boiling captured Sioux. Ma would then fill this with anything she could find that was juicy, and boil it down to a fragrant mouth-watering smell, occasionally including a couple of Sioux the Indians brought in. Bully Belly loved to blow down his soup to cool it, then sloop it. Come early spring, he would blow it north, thawing out the Canadian tundra as far as Yellowknife on Great Slave Lake, occasionally up to Great Bear Lake, and once even to Coppermine on Coronation Gulf. This brought the migrating wildfowl up early. Then he would do his slooping facing south; and many a time the vast Venturi effect of the Torricellian vacuum on the underside of his sloop pulled in a whole flock of geese whose path of migration came too close.

Meantime Dear Ole Ma went about her business in her own usual big way. She was great on cleanliness; and three times a day she would sweep the place

At the Winnebago Reservation near Long Prairie, Paul helped the Indians "bile out the lice".

101

Blanket Indians "sawing wood".

recall, Bunyan had his first logging camp. By now there were camps setting up on the Rum River below Mille Lacs, slowly spreading north and west. It was the idea of the Indian Agent to put these new arrivals to work in Reservation pineries to keep them from getting homesick. The Omega Camp - so called because it was the last place on earth that any man in his right mind would want to be found - was in its third year there when Paul arrived. The first thing he noted was that, among the several hundred Indians in the outfit, not a one had taken a bath in the entire course of employment. In fact, their buckskins were getting so stiff it was hard for most of them to move; and a number had already been sold off as drugstore Indians before it was found they were still alive inside.

Paul immediately set about getting an extra big steel pot to "bile out the lice", as was the wont in camps of his previous acquaintance; and he was particularly fortunate in finding the remains of the steam boiler off the old stern-wheeler *Virginia*, which had so startled the Sioux when it pulled into Ft. Snelling in 1823. Twenty natives were commandeered to haul logs and raise the fire, while another twenty hauled water for "the pot". With his French-Canadian background, Paul naturally called it "de Pot"; and when railroads later became prominent in America, this word "depot" became used for places where the train stops so passengers can clean up.

At a given signal, and when the contents of the huge cauldron were at full boil, every one of the 300 men in camp stripped himself bare and threw the stiff sticky stuff in. A huge noxious cloud arose, only partly composed of steam; and within less time than it takes to tell the story, every man in camp including Paul was gassed into a coma which dropped them in their tracks till next Tuesday.

Meantime a tremendous storm, probably triggered by the ascending cloud of contaminated steam, quenched the fire and stopped the boil. On the second day, with limp and comatose bodies still draped across an acre in every direction, the contents of "de pot" began to set up in the form of a horrendous gelatinous mass. That night petrification set in; and by the time of the general awakening on the afternoon of the third day, every garment in camp was encased in solid rock - which must forever remain one of the world's most famous geological peculiarities. Petrified wood from the Cretaceous Period of 35,000,000 years ago? Yes. But petrified shirts, pants, sox, and Sears Roebuck long-johns??

In the midst of their naked consternation, the everready Paul suddenly remembered the blanket each man had on his bunk; and considerably urged by an early spring chill in the air, the entire camp transformed almost immediately into a blanket brigade. Then, since they were already three days behind in their work, each immediately grabbed a saw and headed into the woods.

In fact, with pay day coming, and the size of the chit depending upon the number of board feet to their credit, every man among them stayed on the job right into the night. Then, because they found themselves already wrapped in their blanket, they saw no point in going home to sleep. So they just stayed there and continued to saw, standing up, wrapped in a blanket - sound asleep.

Therefore, to wit, and to this very day, it is a part of our great American lexicon to say that a man is "sawing wood" when he is sound asleep!

People also wonder about the origins of the buffalo, and particularly its funny name.

When Paul first arrived in Minnesota, and before either Beautiful Legs Benson chased them to death or Gazonk's Flying Clams ate them up, huge herds of two different kinds of beeflike animals literally trampled flat the grasslands of Minnesota plains running south from Long Prairie and west to Duluth. Both were buff-colored; but the one species ran forward while the other ran backward. It accordingly became rather natural to call the ones running toward you *Hellos*, and the ones running away *Goodbyes*.

When Paul arrived with his Blue Ox, the two of them presented a scene that was simply too much for these animals. The entire shoot-luke immediately took off, and in such violent fashion as to bring out this marked distinction between the two species. That is, the buff-Hellos didn't get very far away because they had to run backwards forwards, while the buff-Goodbyes simply disappeared over the horizon, such that none has ever been seen since.

With nothing left but the buff-Hellos, one can see that the course of a mere few years was sufficient to corrupt the name to *Buffalos*.

The Indian's *Kechi-Nijo-Odonima* or Great Bimouthed Squup about to slide a "porky pig" down his gut bypass.

Speaking of vanished species reminds one of that great predator of porcupines that took up habitation on Isle Royale in Lake Superior after Paul made that island during his honeymoon. Remember? This animal was called *Kechi-Nijo-Odonima* by the Indians, or the *great bi-mouthed squup*. The animal had two *odonima* or mouths, hence the name; and each was equipped with a full set of teeth. The upper he used for normal eating; and this connected directly as usual with the stomach. But the lower was for its special diet of porcupines; and it bypassed the stomach and upper colon to make direct connection with the lower bowel. Mother Nature with her usual beautiful forethought arranged this so the quills of the porcupine wouldn't get in nasty positions going around all the usual bends.

But as with so much of Minnesota ecology, the arrival of Paul Bunyan and his weird family caused vast upsets. In the case of the Great Bi-mouthed Squup, all of those alive on Isle Royale at the time took one look at him and headed for the hills. Their demise and eventual extinction then came about in a quite

curious way: The hilltop porcupine supply ran out. This then led to dis-use of the bypass gut, which accordingly began to shrivel and dry. As it did so, it pulled the two ends of the animal together until it looked like an armadillo; whereupon they all eventually rolled down the hills and drowned in Lake Superior.

Most immediate of all extinctions incident to arrival of the Bunyans was that of the famed *pivot-divot*. A much-beloved bird of the Plains Indians, the pivot-divot had just one leg, but with toes and toenails full-circle so that you could never really tell which way it was facing. Also, its neck was swiveled so it didn't make any difference anyway. In fact, the main problem of the pivot-divot was that the critter itself never knew whether it was coming or going.

So when Paul emerged out of the woods with Babe the Blue Ox on that fateful journey from Maine to the Minnesota Northwest, the only three pivot-divots alive at the time took one look at the incredible sight, then attempted instantaneous flight in all directions at once. This, of course, brought im-

103

mediate extinction to the entire species. Feathers were everywhere. Paul thought it was just an early fall of snow, so really never got to know the pivot-divot; and we ourselves would never know about it if some of the Indians had not earlier trained one for use on their golf course, then stuffed it when it died.

Last of the pivot-divots.

CHAPTER XII

END OF THE LINE

So where are they now? Or what happened to them – the illustrious Bunyan Family, that is?

Few if any historians have ever satisfied the whetted Bunyanophile's appetite by telling us what came next after Minnesota, and especially after Oregon. As we shall learn in a sequel volume, Paul was probably driven out of Minnesota by the great legendary folk-hero of the Ojibwe, *Nana-bozho*, when the Indians finally got sore over what Paul did to their beloved Minnesota woods. At last Paul apparently found his match. A few such as the notable poet Robert Frost suggested he went from the West Coast to Alaska after Babe died. But this is all mere hearsay.

While we have only sketchy information brought back by field geologists studying rock formations, and archaeologists collecting weird stories on our progenitors, the situation can be reconstructed roughly as follows:

First, Beautiful Legs Benson simply ran so much he finally went to where he couldn't come back; and Bully Belly B'Hoy, foolishly knocking off a whole wagonload of prunes just because it happened to be standing unguarded at camp, apparently slid to the same place. Bully had always loved prunes; and it was he who was largely responsible for the famed "prunestone chipmunks", which grew so large from eating the seeds he spit out, that they finally got voracious and wiped out all the bobcats east of the Rockies after Bully died. Local residents of Leech Lake still tell of the time they used these chipmunks to chase away the wolves before the overgrown critters finally went west.

Gazonk continued for some time to show signs of a brilliant future. Hearing his father tell about the hootpeckers, he developed his own cross between woodpeckers and homing pigeons for the Wells Fargo Express, the Western Union Telegraph Company, and the U.S. Signal Corps. These wonderful birds would not only deliver a message, but would knock on your door.

He also invented uranium stainless steel buckshot for hunters, using the "spent" or "depleted" uranium-238 left over from atomic reactors. This

looked simply great for awhile, because the uranium made the shot almost twice as heavy as lead. You never had to pick the B-B's out of your roast bird because they went right on through, until the whole flock came down on the first shot. And you could shoot them from Minnesota while they were still in

Gazonk's famed Homing Pecker delivering a message.

Minnesota duck-hunter firing into the Northern Flight with Gazonk's super-heavy U-238 buckshot.

needed a little daytime surgery on the neck of a hoot owl – which didn't give a hoot what you did with his neck so long as he was asleep when you did it. The hourly clicking did become a bit of a nuisance, as the owl slowly pivoted to keep his eyes turned away from the Sun in the daytime; but the sudden snap at sunset as he prepared himself for chow pinpointed the end of the day. Although astronomers didn't particularly care for Gazonk's attitude in giving their profession to the birds, he did come up with some very fine data on the timing of the vernal equinox for purposes of spring planting. This bird remained useful for years, until it unhappily chased some juicy young ptarmigan north of the Arctic Circle, then wrung its own neck when rotating a full 360°. Gazonk had only trained it to twist as far as the summer solstice at latitude 46°N.

Most disastrous of Gazonk's inventions was his *beemuskeet*, sometimes called the *bumblemos*. This started out well, and he was merely following a lead he got from one of his father's own tales about an attempt to stop a mosquito epidemic with bumblebees. The Minnesota mosquitoes have always made history whenever and wherever history has been written, because they get so big you can almost talk to them man-to-man. At the time now in question they were attaining such horrendous size that their shadows interfered with Gazonk's suntanning. So

Canada, without waiting for the Northern Flight.

But of course the recoil was something else. It was bad enough to endure the nuisance of wearing a mattress strapped to one's butt, but it was just too expensive to have to buy a one-way bus ticket back from Iowa for each shot. The whole idea then got shot in the pants after 1903 when the Wright brothers invented airplanes, and hunters had to take out a pilot's license and get air-lane clearance for that first leg of their trip into Iowa.

To satisfy his beloved brother Bully Belly's inordinate desire for honey – before Bully downed the prunes, of course – Gazonk crossed honeybees with lightning bugs so they could gather the stuff both day and night.

Apparently the historic *upland trout* of the Winnibigoshish area were also of his doing; though we have no record on how he got them to come out of the streams and nest in trees.

Bemidji will ever be grateful to Gazonk. For when Brainerd sent all its rats up there, and the Pied Piper of Hamline University couldn't even get them to take a bath in Lake Bemidji, let alone drown, Gazonk solved the problem very easily and in a most scholarly manner. First, he wrote them all letters telling them where to go and how to get there. These letters he then greased with smelly cheese and tossed them into their holes. After a rather short period of time the letters were ". . . duly read and the contents inwardly digested"; whereupon the rats got the message and scrammed[1].

In the field of astronomy Gazonk made his big mark by developing the *ratchet owl*. This merely

Bio-astronomer Gazonk's Ratchet Owl locating the equinoxes.

The frightful Minnesota Beemuskeet pondering its choice between sorghum molasses and *blood*.!

with Dad's help, he managed to capture some bumblebees that were also very large. In fact they had to strap down their wings and put their stingers in a knapsack in order to get them back to camp.

Unfortunately, it was the time of the full Moon; and when Paul and Gazonk unloaded the monstrous bees to attack the mosquitoes, they made love to them instead. Within days this mating of *hymenopterous* with *dipterous* gave birth to the dread *bumblemos* or *beemuskeet* having stingers at *both* ends! Paul immediately ordered three tank-cars of sorghum molasses from Louisiana, which he dumped in a swamp behind the bunkhouse of his Camp; and whenever the loggers came in from cutting, most of the terrible insects pulled themselves apart because of one end wanting molasses, while the other end wanted blood. Some simply got stuck in the sorghum during the argument. Gazonk suggested they save one pair to drill holes in their maple trees for tapping

sap; and Paul agreed – though he first clipped off their kissers so there'd be no hanky-panky, with more kids.

Gazonk, as with most geniuses, burned out early, rather than living a long life; and one fine June day when trying to figure out a Rubic Cube, he simply blew a fuse. He could do it easily enough by three passes of his hand when looking straight at it, but it fouled him up for a full minute when he tried to do it behind his back. It was just more than a brain like Gazonk's could take. Paul and 'Che Washi sadly but proudly offered his brain to scientists, to be pickled and preserved for study and admiration by future generations; but the scientists all declined because they already did that to Einstein's brain. It would be terribly embarrassing to have Gazonk's in a glass washtub alongside Einstein's in a mere Mason jar.

Dear old *'Che Washi Wobble* didn't last much longer either. After the demise and/or disappearance

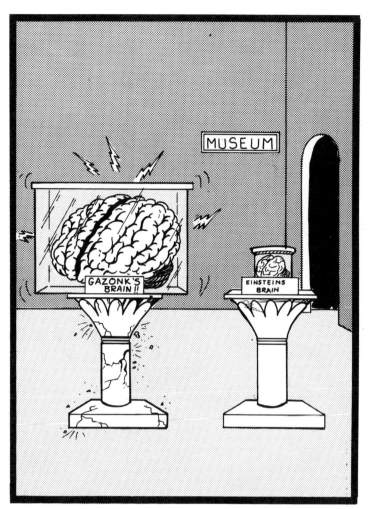

The sad might-have-been museum displays, but for jealousy.

Caucasus, and the Khyber Pass into Asia – possibly even the noted Karakorum Pass of the Himalayas. But there it stops. No Chinaman ever heard of Paul Bunyan.

However, they sure heard of him in Iowa.

For it seems that Paul and his old Scandihoovian pal Beermug Sveeggen took a few steps south one early spring to thaw out their Minnesota chilblains and pick up a little Iowa tan. Getting hungry, Paul decided to plant the kernel of Windigo corn that he got from an Indian friend during a Leech Lake Pow-Wow. The Windigo is the Ojibwe's pet nightmare monster; and to this day the lake by that name in the center of Star Island on Cass Lake marks the place where one spit out an old Indian squaw because she was too tough. When the Ojibwe first saw Paul, they dove into the brush thinking he was the Windigo; but they finally came back out when they saw him bowing and scraping one day before 'Che Washi Wobble, hat in hand, and a foolish look on his face that couldn't possibly belong to a Windigo.

But the corn kernel was for real, from a real monster, and was supposed to grow like one. Paul stuck his thumb in the rich Iowa soil – which by the way, used to be in Minnesota 'till the melt run-off of the Great Ice Ages washed it all into Iowa; then he tossed the kernel into the 4-foot hole and stamped it down.

Ping! PONG!! There was a sharp snap as the sprout broke through the shell, and a much louder report when it hit the bottom of Paul's foot before he had stopped tamping the hole. Up went the stalk. Paul

of her three-thirds of a kid(s), she decided to take up belly-dancing again to restore the vigors of her youth. But instead, all that happened was that she flew apart. Stuff that she shook one way simply didn't come back. Paul sadly mopped up the terrible mess – and that was that, I guess.

With all of his family except Babe now gone, and most of Minnesota logged off, it was time either to fade away or go west. Perhaps the Red Lake Council of Ojibwe Indians is right, and *Nana-bozho* did to him what they claim. For there is no question about Paul going west, also his being very pooped-out when he did. For he was dragging his butt so badly when trying to cross the eastern Rockies that he knocked the peaks off to form the famous South Pass of the later Oregon Trail, between the Laramie and Wasatch Ranges. When he hit the Sierra Nevadas, the same thing developed the Donner Pass. Brother! Was he pooped! While nobody seems to know it, Paul's historic trek did become memorialized by Russell, Majors, and Waddell when they ran their famed Pony Express over the route, and again later by the Union Pacific Railroad.

In fact, there is a clique of history-minded geologists in some of our midwest schools who believe they can further trace Paul's post-Minnesota wanderings by the St. Bernard, Simplon, and St. Gotthard Passes in the Alps; the Daryal in the

Dear ol' Beermug Sveeggen on his way up and out with the Windigo cornstalk in Iowa.

yelled at Beermug to shinny up the dam thing and cut off the top before it got too big. By the time Beermug leapt into action, however, the top was already out of sight. Yet up he went – until he was also out of sight.

"BEERMUG! Wot heppen'd?" yelled Paul. Back came a faint and very distant voice:

"Top no bin har! She grow too fast. Yee - YEEE!!"

And that was the last anybody ever heard of Beermug. Paul always insisted he told Beermug to come back down, and that he tried valiantly to do so. But the corn was growing so fast that for each step the Big Swede took down, he went two steps up.

In a desperate effort to get Beermug back on Earth, Paul laid to with his mighty 6-bit ax, which took deep cuts on every swing E-W, N-S, and up-down. But the cornstalk was growing so fast that he could never produce a chip from a V-cut. By the time the blade came in for the second swing, the last bite was so far up as to be out of sight. Even the clouds were having trouble: They either had to go around or split, because they couldn't go over.

Finally in an act of desperation, Paul pulled up the tracks of the Rock Island Railroad, made a quick hairpin bend at each end of the 103-mile line, whipped a fast knot around the base of the stalk, dropped the hairpin ends into Babe's harness, then gave the poor old ox such a helluva kick in the butt that he went clean over the horizon like a dash of bitters. This pulled the knot into a fatal tourniquet; and down came the cornstalk. But it required a little over three days for the fall to complete itself because of its size. Violent storms swept the whole Mississippi Valley, the remains of which haven't died away yet. But most of the damage was done toward the west in the direction of fall. A former mountain range in Kansas, for example, was knocked so flat that the whole State has ever since served as an emergency landing strip for transcontinental planes that get in trouble.

Did we say flat? Manalive! It was knocked flatter than the pancake Poison Ivitch used to make out of Swedish *knäcke brot*. (His recipe was enough to make them flat, but they were even flatter because Ivitch could never understand Swedes.) In Utah, the huge post-glacial Lake Bonneville got slapped so hard that everything was knocked out of it except the salt – leaving what we now call Great Salt Lake. In California, even the Earth's crust was broken, producing what is today called the San Andreas Fault. But it was really Paul's Fault. May the people who gave it the name be forgiven by San Andreas when they get into heaven – if they ever do.

At this point the trail gets a bit thin because it runs out into the broad expanses of the Pacific. But geologists and oceanographers have discovered a tremendous welt on the ocean bottom which they have named the East Pacific Rise, surrounded by a vast network of cracks which they call the Ring of Fire because it is still volcanically active. Such stuff really adds up.

More definite is the evidence in Hawaii, which apparently got hit by something near the top of the stalk. But to this day it remains unknown whether the big chunk that drove into Mauna Loa to produce the huge crater of Kilauea was an actual cob of corn

The Western Sqonk was so repulsively homely that even his tongue was coated.

grown in such short time on that great stalk or – heaven forbid! – Beermug Sveeggen!

In any event, the State of Iowa has ever since been known as the Tall Corn State – and indeedy-doody, they do come by that title honestly.

Meantime on the trek west out of Minnesota, Paul was frequently cheered by meeting some of the animals he enjoyed so much in his youth. The *sqonk*! Dear little *Lacrimacorpus dissolvens*! While this one wept continually like the eastern species, the reason for it was quite different: It was so dam ugly – buck-toothed, cross-eyed, bow-legged, snot-nosed, bag-eyed, triple-jowled, and with coated tongue and bad breath, yet! Having the raccoon habit of dipping its food into water for cleansing, it got to see its own miserable puss reflected in the water every time it went to eat, and it was simply too much.

Paul managed to get one to crawl into his knapsack by blowing his nose and mopping his eyes – no sqonk bait is more powerful than sympathy! Paul swung the sack on his back and headed on across South Dakota. For awhile he thought he was really recovering his strength like old times, because the bag kept feeling lighter and lighter. But then he recalled the earlier experience back east, and peered in his bag. Sure enough! Nothing left but tears. The sad-eyed little critter had completely dissolved away.

Crossing the Badlands, Paul met another old friend, the *goatithro* or *sidehill gouger*, which folk out there also called the *hoofer*, and taxonomists the *Membri inequales declivitatis*[1]. We will recall this

A dam Augerino pulling the cork out of Paul's joy-juice bottle.

hillside animal as having short legs on one side, and long ones on the other, also that there were clockwise and counterclockwise variants, depending upon which way they went around the hill. However, in the Badlands the males were all clockwise, and the females counterclockwise, such that propagation of the species was virtually guaranteed by their continually running into each other. It is difficult to understand why this country was called the Badlands, because it really wasn't all that bad.

In the Wyoming Rockies Paul ran into some beauties; a few he recognized, others were new. Take the *wampus cat*, for example, which was like the ones he knew as a kid in Maine, except that these had a hinged extension somewhat like a pruning hook on their right foreleg. With this they would snatch an eagle right out of the air. Then there was the dread *hoopsnake* which often came rolling down out of the hills at either him or Babe, with tail in mouth, until it struck; but Paul soon found that the best escape was to climb a fence. This slowed up the snake because he had to unwind to get through.

Down in the valleys was the annoying *augerino*, a huge worm with a corkscrew bill which would pull the cork out of Paul's choice bottles of Madeira, then get roaring drunk and stick his twister right in Paul's butt when he was trying to take a nap.

On the shores of the Green River in Wyoming stood some of the *fillyloo* cranes, whose eggs were so light they had to build their nests upside down to keep them from floating out; and these birds spent most of their day in search of a very interesting little fish called the *goofang*. This fish reminded Paul of his old friend the goofus bird, because it always swam

A Wyoming *caccat* or Cactus Cat the morning after a night out with 231-proof *mesquite dew*. Our word "mosquito" comes from this because of its sting.

backward; though in this case it was not to see where he had been, but rather to keep the water out of its eyes.

In one of the deserts west of Wyoming Paul ran into a *cactus cat* for the first time. This *Felis spinobibulosis* had thorns for hair, toenails like a kitchen paring knife, and a forked tail. A nocturnal feeder, "caccat" would make a nightly circuit of some select cactus grove, and slash the bases to get the sap to exude. Then he would leave that grove for several days to let the sap ferment in the sun, while he ripped up another. The result was a *mescal* running 80-proof on weekdays, and over 200-proof on Sundays – pure spirits. One shot, and *caccat* would waltz off into the moonlight, clacking its toenails and buzzing its thorns, hiccuping like something you never heard

before, and simply screaming with delight. For awhile Paul thought this was kind of funny, but it blew the whole concept of a quiet evening on the desert.

To Paul's inexpressible delight, when he hit the Pacific Coast and found the big Potlatch Camp of Weyerhaeuser, he ran right into his old pal Poison Ivitch or "P.I.", now Head Cook. A celebration was in order; and for old time's sake, they decided to build it around P.I.'s specialty – baked beans. Furthermore, we will recall that both Paul and Babe had been beaned while weaned at the good old Camp on the Androscoggin. The so-called crater of Mt. Lassen, incidentally, was still smoking from Poison's historic Beanhole Bean Day many years before.

And tears now fill our eyes as we write these few closing paragraphs on the biographies of Paul and

Historic last known photograph of Paul Bunyan and his beloved Babe the Blue Ox, taking off from their last great feast on camp beans, baked by none less than their old cook from Penobscot days "P.I." Poison Ivitch, who used the crater of Mt. Lassen for his bean pot.

Babe, for indeed the tale is about to end. Nobody really knows for sure what happened, though the best lead comes from old Doc Slicem, the Potlatch medic. Doc thought that, in view of their age, neither Paul nor Babe had all their valves working. Stable-boy Horsey Hess thought otherwise. He had seen both man and beast eat P.I.'s beans, and in every case it meant courting disaster. The stuff would balloon a steel boiler, let alone an intestine; and on this great feast day both Paul and Babe ate right down to the bottom of Arizona's Meteor Crater, where P.I. cooked them on this occasion.

About 2 a.m., according to the best estimates, both Paul and Babe began lifting off. In a very short time they were completely airborne, and entirely out of reach before Doc could get there with his long thin knife and treat them for the bloats. Up and over the hills they went, off into the black of night – and that is the end of the Paul Bunyan story. It's just that simple, and tragic.

Nothing at all has ever been reported on sighting Paul; and we can only suppose that he may have landed on another planet such as Jupiter, since this would then account for the recent space probes which found this celestial body so full of gas.

Rumor had it at one time that Paul wound up his logging career and went to building ships – rather, a ship, since it became both his first and his last, for reasons that will shortly become apparent. It was a passenger liner; and he named it *The 'Che Washi Wobble* in honor of his deceased wife.

But unfortunately he built it for the Atlantic rather than the Pacific. She was Bunyanesque in size, as one might expect; and the Atlantic simply wasn't big enough or deep enough. She had such tremendous draft she could only float in the San Juan Trench off Puerto Rico. In fact, Paul even had to build the craft there because of objections of Puerto Rican meteorologists. They argued that a bottle of champagne large enough for the launching, while it would have the advantage of producing economic recovery for France, the disadvantage would be a washing away of their inland hills, and irreparable erosion damage to their beautiful beaches. So Paul acquiesced in his usual good-natured way, proceeded to build the ship already in place in the Trench, and simply forewent the christening ceremonies.

However, when she took on her first load, *'Che Washi Wobble's* bottom touched down even in the Trench. Fortunately, she was such a long ship that Paul merely ran a causeway off each end, the one to Brazil and the other to London, thereby creating the First Transatlantic Bridge. In 1927 it was torn down when Charles Lindbergh showed you could do it by air. Paul simply belonged to a gone generation.

Another rumor has it that Paul and 'Che Washi had a daughter called Teeny-Bopper Bunyan. It is said that, although she was of unusually large stature, she did not come through on the installment plan like her three brothers, but instead all at one shot. Teeny-Bopper apparently grew up in one of the Weyerhaeuser camps in northern Oregon, where she invented the skateboard. The account at hand states that there was a huge grove of eggplants near the timberline on Mt. Hood; and in order to keep a good supply of eggs in the cookhouse so that the hungry 'Jacks could enjoy her mother's soft-nose pancakes, Teeny-B. would gather a huge pile, lay a plank across the top, then skateboard them downhill into the camp. This had the additional advantage of delivering the eggs fully scrambled and ready for mixing with the batter.

But we do not believe this to be a dependable record, especially in light of the fact that the skateboard had been invented much earlier by the famed Camp "Vet" Hawk Hallquist, who used to get to his winter work locations by riding a plank down the tote roads on frozen horse apples.

As for Babe, a special international research team is still working on certain mysterious aspects of the so-called *Hindenburg* disaster occurring at Lakehurst, New Jersey, in 1937. It has always been assumed that this was one of Graf Zeppelin's hydrogen-filled dirigibles that blew up and burned on that fateful occasion; but there is a long and lingering suspicion among lumberjacks, and particularly those at the Potlatch Camp who saw Paul and Babe take off, that the Lakehurst explosion might have been Babe. They reason that, being younger than Paul and having the constitution of an ox, Babe's valves may have been a bit more operable. Perhaps he had degassed enough for re-entry, but hit a lightning storm over New Jersey which ignited his exhaust, the combustion then traveling at explosion velocities up the main channel.

For after all, names are often misunderstood and confused, particularly by newspaper reporters; and might it not be that the word *Hindenburg* they thought they got for the name of the huge exploding vehicle was actually *Hind End Burn* – Babe's, that is?

REFERENCES

1. Carson, G.: *Fantastic Animals Prowl Tall Timber of Our Mythology*, Smithsonian 3, 20-5 (1972)

EXTRA! EXTRA! EXTRA!

READ ALL ABOUT IT!!!

BANGOR DAILY ENTERPRISE
25 JULY 1984

Archeologists Confirm Paul Bunyan Legend!

INCREDIBLY EXCITING REPORTS OF DIGS AT PAUL'S OLD CAMP 9 ON THE ANDROSCOGGIN.

Archaeologists, historians, and professors from every reputable college in the nation joined the Bangor Institute of Science this past week at a meeting specially called to evaluate the incredibly fascinating 1984 finds at the old logging site believed to be Paul Bunyan's famed Camp 9 on the Androscoggin River. At a level of exactly seven meters beneath glacial till, archaeologist Dr. Prof. J. Wallin--the man listed in the Guiness' *Book of World Records* as having an I.Q. so high that if you cut him in two he'd still be a genius at both ends--came upon a huge iron pot which was obviously the one the 'jacks had used Sundays to "bile out the lice" from their stinking clothes. For one of their socks was still stuck in the pot. Nearby were also clearly discernible postholes marking the typical barricade used to prevent fatal attacks upon the cook. Even the position of Sourdough Sam's stove could be located by the fascinating fact that three floorboards were still stuck and preserved in some rubbery substance which has thus far defied scientific analysis even with the heliospectroscope. Most exciting of all, however, was the discovery of an enormous tapeworm, judged to be some forty meters in length, whose lower parts had become trapped in "Substance X"--as the gunk is still called.

Immediately two questions become answered by these finds; First, is the famous legend correct in stating that lice in Camp 9 grew to such enormous proportions that a team of 'jacks armed with baseball bats had to stand by on Sundays to keep them from climbing out of the pot? The answer is a resounding "YES!", as so readily proved by Photo A (next page), also the remarkable illustration inside the back cover. For this Photo A

ARCHEOLOGISTS - Continued on page 2.

ARCHEOLOGISTS - Continued from page 1.

shows a **mite** found at the dig--a relatively diminutive cousin of the louse, yet of sufficient size to make the blood run cold in a bobcat. The other photograph displays the renowned suffocated louse found in 1949 in Paul Bunyan's sock so long displayed in the National Museum (courtesy AP Laserfoto).

Second, could it be true that Sourdough Sam's sourdough was invested with such stunning properties as to change the course of Darwinian evolution in some species? And again the answer is an unqualified "YES!", as clearly proved by Photo B showing the **Sourdough Sam tapeworm.** Whether this worm actually crawled out of Sam, or arrived later from some other place, is not yet known.

At the afternoon session on Thursday, folklorist Dr. Zapoof of Harvard University created a near-panic by leading a live Camp 9 bedbug into the room on a leash. He had found it hiding behind a tree, probably still waiting for the 'jacks to come back after Paul blew the place down asking for the gravy. Photo C is the tragic picture which captured the very instant that the creature broke its leash and was preparing to jump. Services for the photographer will be held tomorrow at 2 p.m.

Finally, Professor Rufus Meyers of Wellesley College presented Photo D, described as the head of a montrous **pinworm** which her team of archaeologists had found protruding from the mummified butt of some unfortunate 'jack who had apparently been unceremoniously buried "lumberjack fashion". Supposedly the worm was coming up for air, but couldn't quite make it and got stuck. As with the tapeworm, this is only a head view, since the length of film in a movie camera would not suffice to capture its long skinny body. Professor Meyers reported that she traced it from the burial site in Section 11 until she finally entered Section 36; and since this is the Section in each Township assigned by Congress to schools, she decided to leave it there and let the kids play with it--perhaps for skipping rope.

PHOTO A

Photograph of a **Bunyan Mite,** diminutive cousin of the **Bunyan Louse,** found still roaming around at the old logging site of Bunyan's Camp 9 on the Androscoggin River in Maine.

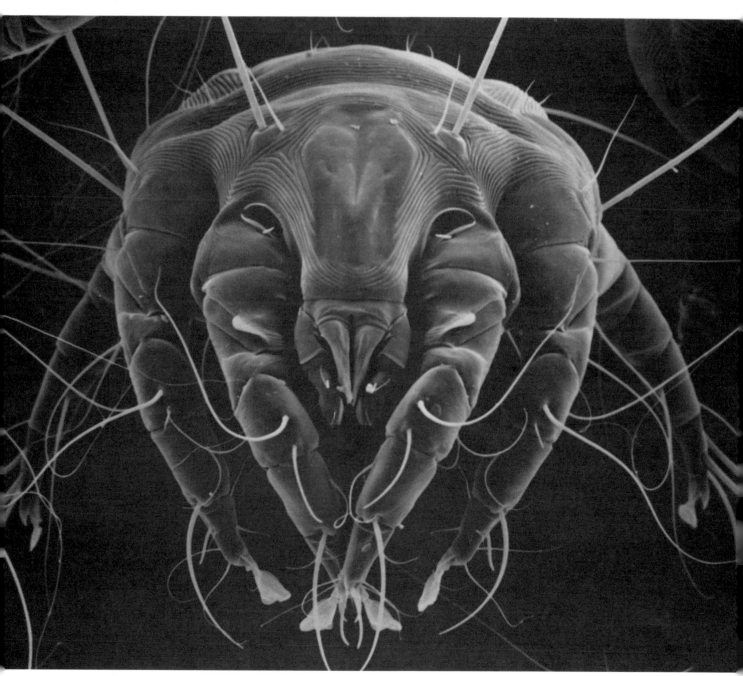

SEM (Scanning Electron Microscope) photograph of a mite found on a hedgehog, magnified 1000 times. Courtesy Science Photo Library, London, and Dr. Tony Brain.

PHOTO B

Intestinal Tapeworm--head only--found still stuck in "Substance X" of Sourdough Sam's kitchen floorboards.

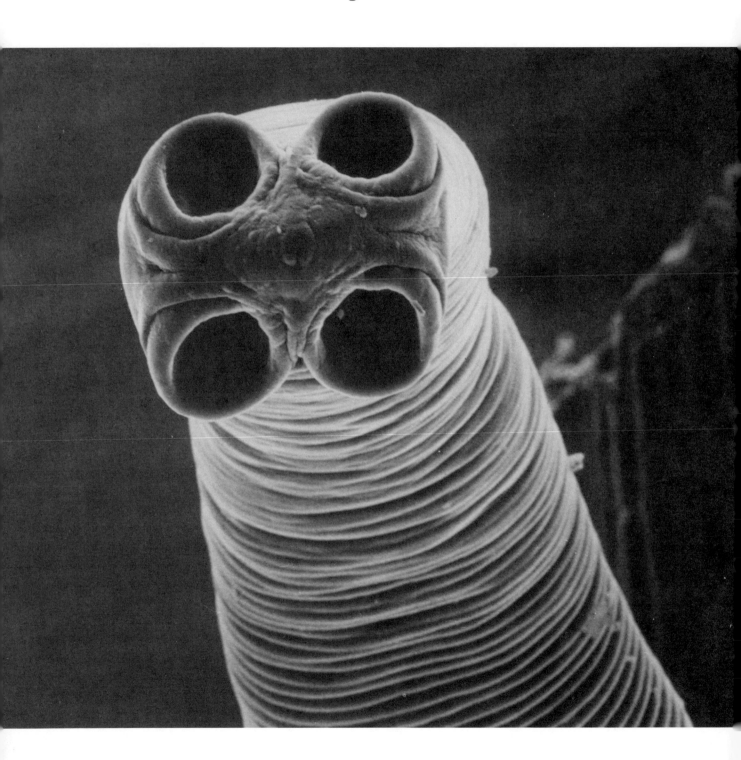

SEM photograph of a large intestinal roundworm at high magnification. Courtesy Prof. John E. Ubelaker and Southern Methodist University.

PHOTO C

Tragic photograph of fearsome **Bunyan Bedbug** captured alive at the Camp 9 archaeological site, and photographed just 3 nanoseconds before finishing off the photographer.

SEM photograph of the bedbug **Cimex sp.** magnified 100 times. Courtesy Prof. John E. Ubelaker and Southern Methodist University.

PHOTO D

Head of the ugly **Pinworm** found in a left-over carcass of some unfortunate lumberjack at Bunyan's Camp 9.

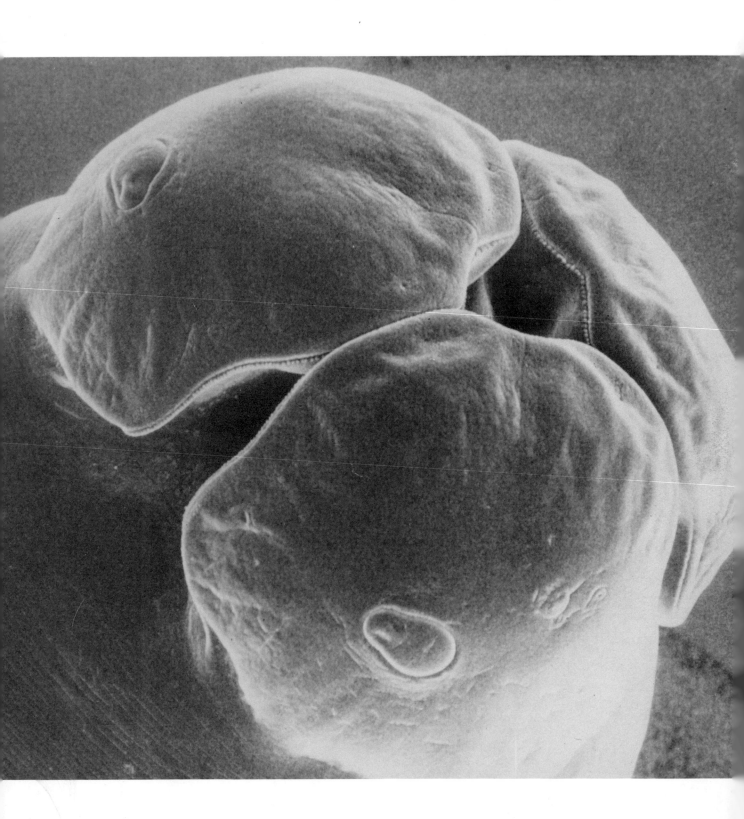

SEM photograph of the head of a **Pinworm** showing teeth and eye-type sensors at high magnification. Courtesy Prof. John E. Ubelaker and Southern Methodist University.